YOU ARE NOT WHO YOU BELIEVE YOU ARE

THE BIG LIE

TERRY L. NEWBEGIN

NEC PRESS

Published by NEC Press
Tennesee, USA

Copyright © 2021 by Terry L. Newbegin
All rights reserved.

No part of the book may be reproduced by any mechanical, photographic, or electronic process, or in a phonographic recording. The book will not be stored in a retrieval system, transmitted, or otherwise copied for public or private use other than for "fair use" as brief quotations embodied within the book without prior written consent from the author.

The author does not dispense medical advice nor prescribe the use of any technique as a form of treatment for physical or medical problems without the advice of a physician, either directly or indirectly. The author is only offering information as a unique nature to help in your quest for clarity, health, abundance, and joy. If you use the information or techniques in this book for yourself, which is your constitutional right, the author and the publisher assume no responsibility for your actions or any of its results.

Book Cover and Interior Design by Monkey C Media
Edited by Nancy Salminen

First Edition
Printed in the United States of America

ISBN: 978-1-7356947-2-6 (Trade Paperback)
ISBN: 978-1-7356947-3-3 (Ebook)

Library of Congress Control Number: 2021912300

I dedicate this book to my son,
Toby Newbegin,
who transitioned from Earth to the realms of Sovereignty and Freedom on January 20, 2021. My son Toby was an adventurer, an experiencer of life, a proud served Navy man, and a student of ancient civilizations and its history. Toby enjoyed riding his motorcycles, watching sports, and looking after his two daughters. Toby was always a student of spirit, and when he left Earth, he made a point to channel a message to his loved ones.

CONTENTS

Acknowledgment 3
Author's Commentary... 5
We Are Programmed Humans... 14
My Beginning 20
Life After Bankruptcy... 27
My Next Adventure.. 34
Reincarnation 43
The Four Building Blocks of God 57
The Garden of Eden... 69
Belief Systems 77
The Ego Seized all Power and Control... 86
The False God 95
Religion 102
Our Reality Is Based on Lies.. 120
Knowing that You Are Christ, God, and a Goddess 127
Exploring Heaven and Hell 136
Stealing Energy 145
The Myth of Putting Others First... 154
Memories 163
Learn How to Remove Your Chains 175
The Big Lie!... 180
Epilogue 195

*If,
for some reason,
you have picked
up this book and are now glancing
over its contents, then know that this
means there is something within you
that is beginning to awaken.
The big question is,
are you ready
to take the next step
in your discovery?*

ACKNOWLEDGMENT

With a celebrated gratitude and heartfelt thank you, it has been a special honor for me to serve as a conduit for Yeshua Ben-Joseph (known as Jesus), Lord Melchizedek, Mother Mary, Mary Magdalene, Tobias, Moses, Abraham, Methuselah, Adamus Saint-Germain (known as Samuel in the Old Testament), Kuthumi Lal Singh (known as Balthazar, one of the wise men who came to honor the birth of Jesus), and Saint Dominic. And since Yeshua is well known to many as Jesus, then Jesus will be the name I will use for this material presented.

These wonderful Ascended Masters have gone beyond the confines of human beliefs and incarnations, giving them a broader outlook of God, Goddess, Christ, the Anti-Christ, Cain and the Beast, and whom we all call Satan or the Devil, which they have shared with me. And now, I am pleased, honored, and content to share the message with you.

These Grand Masters from the other side of the veil are eager and overjoyed for those who choose to read the messages contained in this book as it has the potential to open you up to the many lies that we all have been living under for centuries.

I give honor, respect, thanks, and love to my wife Dianna for her patience, support, devotion, and love, giving me space, time, and trust to stay committed to the angelic realm and their objective to awaken those that are ready for a new understanding of life and freedom.

I want to give thanks to an exceptional lady, Nancy Salminen, of Surry, Maine. Nancy's editing and her contribution of endless hours of hard work proved invaluable as she patiently, and with unconditional love and determination, helped make the production of this book possible.

Nancy, I am deeply blessed and honored to have you as a friend and a spiritual companion in this journey. With your editing, you have set the stage for me to express my work in a clear and precise manner. Therefore, I give my gratitude, unconditional love, and appreciation.

AUTHOR'S COMMENTARY

I titled the book "You Are Not Who You Believe You Are" with a subtitle, "The Big Lie," because realistically, you are actually not the person you believe you are. You are not your mind, name, or body. And, if you are not these things, then "Who are you?" Are you not the person born of your parents? What if I told you that the most kept secret about life has never been about as to whom you believe you are, but rather it is about you following the convictions of such dark individuals and a God outside of you that it would possibly provoke you to not wanting to read this book.

For instance, what if I told you that you have been worshipping a God based on the character and behavior patterns of an Anti-Christ, a devil, and that of a Cain consciousness so dark that it may send shock waves right up your spine. Would you believe me, or would you say that I am ridiculously offensive and irresponsible with my words?

What if I mention to you that even the belief that God's working of the State of Israel is actually the creation of such dark forces that just the idea of me making this statement seems inconceivable. In fact, one may say that this statement alone is in complete opposite of what we have been taught about the State of Israel and what we read in the Bible.

What if I tell you that the Bible that we are familiar with has been rewritten and played with over thousands of years to assist these dark-minded individuals worldwide in taking over our minds, our souls, and who we truly are from a spiritual level; thereby, we have become a slave to them. Even what we believe about Rome (Vatican), Israel, the United States, and the Catholic Church has been a place of lies, evil doings, soul stealing, and deception.

And when I learned of this from Jesus and the Ascended Masters in 2004, I was overwhelmingly upset, as it took me a while to comprehend what I was channeling as to its validity. And yes, this is the same Jesus that walked the earth over two thousand years ago. However, another shocking truth is that Jesus is not his real name. His real name is Yeshua Ben Joseph. The name Jesus comes from the Greeks of long ago. If one did any research on the name Jesus, one would find that the name Jesus is far from being a Hebrew name during Yeshua's time on earth.

The most shocking was when I learned that the God in the Bible we seem to worship as a loving God is actually a God of death, destruction, and lies. For example, I have learned that the true God is not about death. The true God is only about life, prosperity, and unconditional love. And this can be seen throughout the universe and beyond as everything is life. Earth is not the only planet with life, and we are not the only species in the cosmos that are of life. Life, like God, is everywhere, including other species from many different galaxies and dimensions, and they have visited us here on earth for centuries.

The proof is all around us, but because of governments, religions and their scholars, and their made-up God of the Bible, we have been fooled and tricked into believing that earth is the only planet with life. However, as time moved forward with the channeling of Jesus (Yeshua) and the Ascended Masters, I began to understand why this information about the real God was given at this time. It's called the "Awakening," as some call it the Harvest!

To keep the reference of Yeshua simple, I will refer to him as Jesus since he is mainly known as that name today. Hence, if you are brave enough to read this book in its entirety about my metamorphosis into the fifth dimension and higher, then you will learn what religions are actually calling Christ return is, in fact, the dark forces keeping you and the world distracted and hypnotized to learning the real truth about Christ's return.

For instance, it is not about Jesus, the man, returning to earth to save us. It is about the "Christ Consciousness" and how it has never left the earth since Jesus, the man, left over two thousand years ago, and we are asleep to it. In other words, Jesus, the man, does not want to be worshipped because it is not about him. It is about the "Christ Consciousness."

As you read through the channeled material within this book, I have laid out some of the most profound messages that have come from Jesus and the Ascended Masters that will either provoke you, shock you, or awaken you to the certainty of Jesus and how he is not returning to earth to save you or anyone else. So, buckle your seat belt because you are about to learn "who you truly are" and how you and the world's population have been tricked and programmed into following the Anti-Christ for over sixteen thousand years.

Without realizing it, just about every choice you make in life today is controlled by our governments and religion's dark forces and their leaders and followers, including your free will to choose. And I am speaking of choices that guarantee these dark individual supporters of soul-stealing that no matter what you decide, ninety-seven percent of the time, you will end up choosing precisely what they want you to choose, even right down to what you eat, what you buy, how you are educated, who to vote for, and what you believe about Jesus, God, and the Devil. Does this surprise you? It did me!

To help you understand more of what Jesus and the Ascended Masters are talking about, they have presented this material from the idea of you being a divine human and not you just being a human. But because of brainwashing, you have been following a side of you that is so overwhelmed with fear that it causes you to become traumatized to where you just cannot accept that you are Christ and the savior of you and your world in which you live. Instead, you follow the dark forces by default. And you thought you were nobody of importance!

Well! We have not been following Christ or the words of Jesus since he left because we have been too busy worshipping the man and his demise on the cross instead of his message about Christ. Doesn't it seem odd to you that most of us on earth have been worshipping the messenger instead of the message? Do you really believe that Jesus wants your worship? No! Jesus wants you to study, learn, and awaken to the Christ within you as he did.

We all have been following the words of the dark forces and how they have steered our consciousness on worshipping Jesus, the man, instead of the Christ ideal. Of course, let us hope that this book will help awaken you and those that are ready and willing to do some self-study in what Jesus, the Ascended Masters, and I are trying to reveal to you in this book. And that is, you are a Christ also!

I know many of you may be thinking, what the hell is he talking about? In fact, you may even be saying to yourself that there is no way anyone can make me follow the Anti-Christ, or for that matter, who to vote for without me knowing it? Well, allow me to ask you a few questions. Are you wearing a mask, or did you wear a mask during the COVID 19 era? How about the experimental vaccine shot? Because if you have gotten the shot without doing any research behind the real motive, then you have been following the Anti-Christ for a very long time.

What's been hidden from us is that we, the people of this earth, have been locked into a programmed consciousness where these dark-minded heartless individuals, called our politicians and church leaders, have been controlling every aspect of our lives for centuries, even how we all accepted and chose to believe in a God of death and destruction instead of a God of life, sovereignty, and freedom.

The perfect example of this is Jesus on the cross, as we still today worship this image of a man on a cross instead of revering and idolizing his message. These dark souls do not care if they are involved in thousands of deaths, the ruining of millions of lives and businesses, or the ruining of nations, as long as they are in control of you, your soul, and the world in which you live. Yes, the God and the message of Christ that we worship today has been taken over and has been controlled by these heartless souls since God's inception, as we are very much asleep idolizing a false God that is solely based on duality, lies, power, manipulation, right, wrong, judgment, hate, envy, destruction, and greed.

The creation of religions eons ago by these dark-minded souls was to create a God that we would buy into to control every aspect of our lives. And we all fell for it without question or study! Just like we are doing with the COVID 19 and its miracle shot. Of course, many ask, then who are these dark-minded humans, and why would they want to control us? The answers lie with our politicians, our banking system, our religions, the media, the elites, and those self-proclaimed college professors who declare themselves as our moral compass.

All of them work hard to control every aspect of your thinking to keep you asleep to the real Christ. And they do it at any cost necessary, even if it means death to most of the population. Compared to the billions of people in this world, there are just a handful of individuals who control the billions, and they do it by creating the illusion that we, the people, are in charge of our lives and that we need a savior. And yet, it is all an illusion, and it has been going on for centuries.

But there is hope because the world has been inundated since 2004 by many Ascended Masters from beyond the physical veil joining up with other Masters here on earth in the flesh to help raise the consciousness frequency for those that are ready to hear the real truth about themselves, Jesus, and the Christ consciousness. This will cause those who are willing to awaken to ascend to the fifth-dimensional consciousness. Thus, leaving behind the three-dimensional consciousness of sin, pain, and suffering, to where one becomes a sovereign being.

So, the question is, how do we overcome this deception of being free and sovereign people? It comes down to self-study, deep breathing, and then realizing that *"You are not who you believe you are."* And once you come into some realization of what you believe as to the "free will" to "choose," that of positive and negative energy as being real, and how this dual-energy displays itself through the playing of opposites, then that will be the first step in your awakening to this fifth-dimensional consciousness.

Many of you have worked so hard for centuries to understand what is light and dark, good and evil, right and wrong, without fully understanding their effects on your choices, sovereignty, and your freedom. In fact, without question, you place your heart and soul on what you believe is right and wrong and that you must choose between one or the other if heaven happens to be part of your vision. Well! That is part of the big lie placed on you because of the love for money, political parties, religion, power, and control.

Because of family traditions based on indoctrinated beliefs by those in power, we remain asleep to the real Christ, the real God, and who we indeed are at our core. My friends, we have been misled by many that have taught us that right and wrong is our moral compass when it comes to following good or evil, and if we do not adopt this truth, we are then destined to retribution and hell forever. Without realizing it, we have been compelled to believe that light and dark (good and evil) are real. But on a deeper spiritual level, let it be known that light and dark are all part of the deception and the lies told to us by those that love to keep us blind to the real Christ.

For instance, most believe that our mind is the only source that shapes the reality that we live. We believe, and without question, that we are our name, our accomplishments, our family history, our education, our intelligence, our religion, and our occupation. Well! We are far more than those things! We have forgotten over many generations that we have handed over our sovereignty, free will, and our choices to those that love directing us as if we are cattle for them to feed.

For example, before I came to my awakening, I actually believed that my mind, and the name given to me by my parents, was who I was, nothing more. I even believed in a God that came from a mental perception of what I thought God should be, and therefore I followed this God without question. However, since I have been channeling Jesus and the Ascended Masters from beyond the physical veil since 2004, and from my many encounters with them, the message is very clear; we are far more than just a human here on earth needing to be saved.

My friends, it is not about sin or being saved. It is that we, according to Jesus and the Masters, are the God of light and the Christ consciousness that created all that we see and experience today, including this false God we seem to follow and worship, as well as those of the dark that are running our world today out of fear. Allow me to give you a great example of what the Masters are speaking about when it comes to the real God.

Everyone seems to know about the "Tree of Life" mentioned throughout the Bible, Genesis 2:9, and how it relates primarily to the operation of our super-subconsciousness, our subconsciousness, and our outer ego-personality consciousness and how each consciousness allows us to play in many physical lifetimes being fed by a "universal principle of life and light" that comes from the wisdom of our super-subconsciousness (or the Christ within). Then through evolutional consciousness growth, as in trial and error (karma), we eventually produce the same leaves as the "great tree," which is our own "I AM" Christ Consciousness.

Know that our Spirit and or Christ consciousness is a higher version of our mind and ego consciousness. Thus, wherein we humans together are the individualized portion of the "Spirit of One." It is that we humans are a Goddess and a Christ unto ourselves, and we have forgotten that we are part of a "universal omnipresent measureless mind field of pure unadulterated neutral energy," which is an energy that is present everywhere at once that we use for our creations, even though it seems like we are dealing with dual-energy.

Therefore, the composition of our Spirit (or Christ consciousness) is that we are; (i) an "I AM" individualized God-Goddess unto ourselves, (ii) we are known as having an extraordinary intelligence that comes from out of our Christ Consciousness, (iii) we have a soul that takes on growth patterns to learn wisdom, (iv) we are a divine being that is gifted with free will that cannot be changed, but can be stolen, (v) our "I AM" Spirit is the creator of all energy, including dual-energy, and (vi) we have such a divine passion for venturing outside of ourselves and our neutrality, that we actually ended up creating a mind of perception that activated multiple ego personalities of self to experience all possibilities of life, good and bad, light and dark. And yet, it is all an illusion because, in reality, these "six divine attributes" represent the six days of creation.

It is from these "six divine attributes" that make all of us a Christ and a God-Goddess unto ourselves, and not that this God of the Bible created us or that we must worship. Worshipping comes from our mental perception of things as truths and the belief in a God of power, destruction, and control. However, because of these "six divine attributes" as part of all souled beings, even those souls with dark intentions, we are still part of the Christ consciousness, also known as the "Spirit of One."

It is just that we are very much asleep to whom we are, and therefore, we exist through an ego-personality called the Cain consciousness that believes in power, money, control, and dual-energy as our God.

And that is the God-Devil that these dark-minded souls placed in the Bible as our God and Devil a long time ago. However, know that regardless of what family tree we were born into here on earth, we all remain a member of the Spirit of One (or the wholeness of the Christ consciousness), no matter how far we fall into the darkest pit of forgetting our true heritage.

This is what happened to those lost, cruel-minded souls that are now playing with a consciousness so evil that it makes those we say are bad seem respectable and fair from the outside. We, and those of the dark, have forgotten that we all carry within us "all that the Father-Mother God-Goddess have," for we, as a souled being, are the Father-Mother, Son, and Holy Spirit. We are gifted with free will; we are absolute, infinite, and we are not just the creator of our own world and our experiences here on earth. We are also the creator of the universe and all that is physical, including our human body. Even those who have chosen to follow dark evildoers and their version of God, we all have played a part.

In other words, we, as a Christ also, hold all authority and power of the wholeness of creation because we are a portion of the wholeness of Spirit, meaning no one has more or less authority or power than another, not even the angels we believe come from a higher dimension. However, we can be tricked into believing that one has more power than another, thus giving away our authority as a creator and as a Christ. And that is what these dark-minded humans did to us on an immense scale, and in the process, stealing our consciousness, the free will to choose, and our soul for the benefit of controlling every aspect of our life.

By allowing those souls of destruction to trick us into giving away our free will, our power, and creative ability as a Christ also to them, we became their puppets to do with as they please. And this is what is going on today, as most of the world population is asleep in knowing one is God and the Christ savior who is to come and save the world. Therefore, know that nothing exists outside of your core essence as a Christ that is physical, mental, and declared as power, including the man Jesus because all of what is outside of you is just an illusion. This also includes the person you believe you are in the physical.

Nothing is real other than your consciousness and the energy you use for your creations. And even then, this energy is not real if it is taken up as dual-energy, good and bad. Not even what you call sin is real! Or what most of us call "God's day of rest" is real because the "seventh day," according to Jesus, represents the "seventh attribute" of your Spirit. And this attribute can be confirmed in Genesis, Chapter Two, as the seventh day where God is known to rest. However, the real meaning behind the seventh day is that of (vii) "silence."

Therefore, the "seventh day" has nothing to do with God resting but it is about you, as a God-Goddess and a Christ unto yourself, learning to silence your mind before considering to manifest something to experience. We need to "silence" our minds and contemplate what we are choosing to experience, or else we can find ourselves swimming in an earth energy force so dense that it can cause us much pain and suffering. And that is what we effectively did long ago and continually do today.

After all, every one of us is a God-Goddess in our own right. So be careful about what you create for yourself to experience. If you focus only on dual-energy as being real, that your mind is who you are, then you will experience both good and evil. The wisdom is to know that you are equal to God and Christ because you are God and Christ. Therefore, exercise your authority (power) wisely while in the flesh because if you don't, then be prepared to be taken over by others, especially the dark forces. And, if this is hard to accept, then let it be known that you have been spellbound, put asleep, by those heartless humans that love to control your life, soul, and the free will to choose.

Allow your divinity to come to you in the simplest way without you interfering with it. It is only waiting for your invitation and acceptance. Remember the unpardonable sin? It is that of inherent laziness to look within oneself for the answers and not outside of self because all that is outside of self is a perceptional mind waiting to make choices from an emotional level. Thus, you leave your spiritual education, health, joys, and abundance up to all that is outside of you, such as the Church, the media, your teachers, and your politicians. Not a very good idea, to say the least, as we are susceptible to suggestions about what to choose is best for us.

Chapter 1

WE ARE PROGRAMMED HUMANS

Because of being brainwashed and programmed, we have actually forgotten that there is no soul involvement with our free will to choose our actions other than to follow those that programmed us many lifetimes ago. And it still continues today! Why is this? Because everything we think and act on is mental and emotional, which is why we are conditioned and programmed to follow those who teach and believe Christ and God belong to only one man.

If we continue to give up our free will and have no choice because of following others' ideas of God, and if not God, then others' mental perceptions of what life and God should be in their eyes, then our programming will continue. Thus, our suffering not only becomes a big lie but a long-laasting lie. And the best way to get out of that lie is to invite our Oversoul (Christ) back into our life. We have forgotten that our "I AM's" Christ consciousness is our "Oversoul" that brings in all the wisdom of our experiences, from our past lifetimes right on up to our present lifetime.

Therefore, know that your Christ consciousness and your higher awareness are missing in your life when creating your experiences. Why? It is due to the following other's belief systems and your Cain consciousness about who you believe you are and who you are not. When you are awakened, you know that you cannot find truth by using the mind because the mind is a creation of your Christ consciousness. Therefore, all that is required to bring in your Oversoul's wisdom is for your Cain consciousness to move beyond what your perceptional mind tells you about who you should believe outside of your own consciousness.

My friends, we have been tricked and misled because of power, money, and control. And, believe it or not, spiritual laziness is at the top of the list. Remember, laziness can come in many forms, even spiritual laziness. And, because of that spiritual laziness, we are following the will of all those that have come before us that were programmed to believe in an icon of a God that lives in the mind of man and a Book that portrays this God as "all-powerful, supreme, and a God that created us." Therefore, this God must be worshipped at all cost. We all have forgotten about how the Devil is very creative and cunning when it comes to having us follow someone outside of ourselves.

For example, we all have been taught as the word of God to give at least ten percent of our time and money to God. And yet, this ten percent goes to the Church. The message from Jesus is that this ten percent has been misunderstood for centuries. Because the real meaning behind the ten percent is that you need to give at least ten percent of your time seeking out the Christ within yourself. And it is done is through quieting your mind and doing deep breathing.

Since our life has been set up by external events that have nothing to do with "who God and we are," then we have forgotten that we are connected to our human name and our parent's name, our grandparent's traditions, our education, our vocation, our place in society, and most of all, how we are programmed into interpreting our good and bad stories and experiences in life as good and evil, truth and lies. However, let it be known that we all have been inadvertently programmed by the system without us realizing it.

Thus, all choices come from our own beliefs and what the system has designed for us to believe and experience. Some call it the matrix, and some call it socialism, collectivism, and even communism! And if we would feel into our thoughts and beliefs about Christ, our political viewpoints, and to whom we believe and trust without having to explain away our behavior patterns, we would see that these behavior patterns are what defines us as to "who we believe we are today."

If we continue to buy into the definitions of our behavior patterns, then we can excuse almost any action we take, good or bad, by saying, "that is just the way I am," which we are not. Because of dual-energy beliefs, we become baffled about "why are we the way we are" compared to being the creator of "all that we are." It has come down to the living and the dead, interpreted as to those awakened and to those who are asleep!

Those dark-minded souls in power today teach us of a God that can only be known through faith, and those that do not believe in God teach us that their way of thinking is in our best interest. And yet, it is not about having faith in God or their way of thinking about what is best for us that is confusing. It is the application and the image they project on us that is confusing. Therefore, allow me to tell you the story of my awakening in hopes that it will trigger your awakening. Thus, you joining the living!

However, before I begin my story, I would like to explain why I chose to write this book at this time in my life. From my perspective regarding God, the Devil, Christ, and what is in the Bible as to good and evil, and how religions interpret it. I found in my study of these things one should always ask, "Who am I, really?" "Why am I here on earth?" "What is my purpose for living?" "Why do I believe what I believe?" And, "What I do believe, is it the real truth, or is it all just a big lie put in place for me to learn wisdom, or is it to give away my soul and power to others?"

For myself, when it comes to truth or lies, I have always levitated toward my intuitive feelings. Of course, in the beginning stages of practicing with my intuitive consciousness, it seemed that I was choosing things that weren't in my best interest. And yet, I found out later in life that my intuitive feelings were just working out just fine.

You see, ever since I attended High School, I always desired to be my own boss. So, when I graduated, I took what I was taught, what I knew about God and Christ, and what I was taught about the mind being the recipe to reach my life's dreams, and I processed all the wisdom gained in each experience. I even read many positive books, studied the Bible, and saw the movie "The Secret," and I even learned to visualize what I wanted to accomplish in life. But, to my surprise, none of it worked.

Now, why was that? It did not work because I was among the dead, programmed by the system, believing that the mind is the source for all power and that dual-energy and the Bible's God we worshipped was real. And this belief led me to many failures. However, as I moved into the direction of learning who I am and who I am not at my core consciousness, I found in my study of Spirit that it was our religious leaders, our teachers, our parents, our governments, and the media, all through ignorance, that lied to me since the time I was introduced to the system as a newborn. And it is the same with you and everyone else.

Mind you! It was not that I was a victim or that I am blaming the system! It was what I was taught about the mind as being the source and power behind reaching my dreams and how it turned out to be the mind that prevented me from achieving those dreams. You see, it wasn't my mind or what I was taught by others that have made me successful today. It was my Oversoul, or the Christ and the God within, conveying my true beginning and who I truly am at my core consciousness. For example, I was the one who really shaped and laid out my life's plan, and not science, religion, or even this God of the Bible.

Allow me to explain! When studying scripture and revisiting what I was taught in school by the system, it led to asking myself a big question, "Who am I?" This question then led to other questions like, "Why was I born? And "Why earth, and for what purpose?" I even had thoughts about why there is so much suffering in the world. However, my big question was, "Why are God and Christ such a mystery?" And the answer I received, "God and Christ appear as a mystery because we have set ourselves up by the dualistic programmatical system for them to be a mystery."

Without realizing it, my Oversoul has been hiding from me for many lifetimes. And, by choosing to open up my heart and put aside my dogmatic beliefs in all that is of opposing energy for a while, my

Oversoul began to open up to me the whys of choosing the route of sin, playing opposite roles, choosing physicality, choosing brainwashing, forgetfulness (death), and suffering as the means to remember, "who I AM." And, if I believe that I am God and Christ in the flesh, then I AM. It is that simple!

If you believe you are the way you are because of everything you have been taught, then know that is who you are, nothing more, nothing less. When you live and make decisions from the mind of reason, that of logic, judgment, good and evil, and from others' long-established interpretations of "that is the way it is," then your Oversoul cannot bring forth the wisdom you hold deep within your consciousness memories. Thus, you are dead (asleep)! This is why it is so important to learn "who you truly are at your core essence" in this lifetime.

Know that you gave up your free will a long time ago to others who love power, money, and domination without you realizing you even did it. Also, suppose you believe in destiny, that you are a sinner, and you have to belong to a religion or go to Church, or you are unworthy of miracles because of what you think you did. In those cases, you are processing "who you truly are" in an intellectual way, through the rational mind and not through your Christ consciousness.

It is not about intelligence or your ability to be smarter and more powerful than someone else. Or if religion, government, schools, and others know more than you. It is not even how much money you make or how much you know about God, or how much you go to Church. It is about knowing and being aware of your Christ consciousness, who you are following, and how the body and mind relate to your Oversoul's wisdom.

One thing is for sure! It seems we will always choose to suffer because our mind is nothing but the center of mental impressions that are based only on judgment, sin, and thought patterns of good and evil, right and wrong, that carry within them a very dense impenetrable vibrational energy that only perceives us as a male, female, and a human who is unworthy of being a divine expression of the Spirit of One. And this is why we, as a human, perpetuate our truths (lies) because it is all based on other's belief systems as being something real. And this is why we suffer and create the things we experience in life.

For instance: When I was born, there was a brief moment when my human identity was not known to my parents, my brothers, or the world. Then a few minutes later, my parents celebrated my birth by giving me a name. And with that name, I was then introduced to my family, myself, and the world. However, what was unknown to my family and to me was what my story would consist of in this lifetime.

Therefore, to help those that are willing to listen, I have put together a few Chapters explaining more of what I mean about how we, before we enter the earth, create our own story and how we want to play them out. But first, before we begin, we all need to know that our minds generate our thoughts, emotions, ideas, and perceptions and then stores them away as our truths as memories to whom we believe we are, thus leaving out any of those memories belonging to other lifetimes. Thus, as to our parents and their parents before them, we were all born into this world already entranced to what we believe is truth or lies.

Chapter 2

MY BEGINNING

We assume that our beginning of life was when we were born on earth and that our biological parents are the ones that made it happen. For most, like me, I had this belief growing up that I never existed before 1948. However, after reaching the age of curiosity, I began to research the subject, and I uncovered something about myself that most would never consider. I found that my birth here on earth in 1948 was not the first time living here on earth. Why do I say this? To my surprise, what I learned is that I overlooked the importance of my consciousness, my memories of dimensional proportion, and how my reality and experiences had come from them.

I know that this may sound weird, but I did learn that it takes an absolute "act in consciousness" before energy is stimulated enough to bring about any idea or materialism or life before it can be played out here on earth. However, before my awakening to this fact, I first had to be born on earth with a name given to me by my parents to identify me as someone part of the human race. Also, according to my parents, when I was born, I looked as if I was three months old, weighing almost eleven pounds, and yet, growing up, I was thin.

We were a family of seven, including my father and mother, and I was the middle child out of five siblings. The family lived in a small town in Northern Maine where it can get very cold during the winter months. It was also a time in my infant life, where I had no clue that I was even conscious of my existence, let alone being God's creation. After six months to a year living on earth, I learned to recognize my human name as the name I answered to in this lifetime. Thus, it did not take long before I understood and judged my human name as to "all that I was" and that I never existed before 1948. Also, along with that belief, I was taught that good is God's way and evil is the Devil's way, with having no middle ground for misunderstanding or interpretation.

As I entered into the first five grades of public school, I began to develop a certain type of belief that kind of fortified that my given name was indeed who I was as an individual. For example, the first few school grades taught me that certain letters of the alphabet, when put together, formed words; and then those words were shaped into sentences that evolved into paragraphs, pages, and books. As with words, sentences, paragraphs, pages, and books, public schools taught me how to use numbers. And, if applied correctly, I could become a successful person in life.

For example, if I learned and understood numbers, it could get me into a business that could result in joy and abundance if applied correctly. Nonetheless, in my first few years here on earth, I learned to take full responsibility for my actions and be fair when dealing with others. And when it came to religion, I was taught that a loving God created me, Christ died for my sins, and in return, I was to love, honor, and worship him and his son with all my heart and soul as my Lord and savior. And since I was born a Catholic, I was required by the Church to follow through with the Church's sacraments (oaths and rituals).

I even remember when I first learned about the Catholic teachings of the Church. I recall getting excited about going to Church on Sundays. I even recall as an eight-year-old getting up early on Sunday mornings, without my parents or siblings ever knowing about it, running to Church to attend the first mass at 6:00 A.M. and then running back home after mass so I could do it all again with the family. However, beginning in the sixth grade and up, I somehow began to feel very disillusioned with God and the Church, and even what I was taught in school about fairness and responsibility.

Because what I saw and heard back then was that everything seemed to be more about money, who you knew, and what position you held in society. There were many times when I would witness well-to-do kids, their parents, our town authorities, our teachers, our politicians, and even churchgoers advocating what is best for us, but their actions seemed to be very different from their words. From the Church's point of view, it was all about giving money and helping others to the point that we forgot about ourselves.

It was like we had to give so much of ourselves to others and the Church that we eventually lost sight of our own needs. The Church would preach about money being the root of all evil, and yet, it was the Church that kept on asking for more and more of it. So, we were expected to give and give until we had nothing to give anymore. Even with what I saw and heard from our town officials growing up, it did seem, at least from the outside, like they were looking out for the public good. But, behind the scenes, they were just looking out for those that would fill their pockets for them to stay in power. I say this because of how the town ordinances seemed to fit those individuals and companies that supported their next election.

When I began to recognize these inconsistent behavior patterns at a young age, around twenty or so, I also noticed the media, locally and nationally, were all about supporting the views that best matched the views of the system instead of being neutral. So, that was the time when I stopped listening to the news. At least until I was much older. But now, today, I do not watch the media news at all. It wasn't that I was much of a news listener anyway. But, when I did listen, it seemed most of it was very unbalanced and had no common sense to what was being reported.

I know that I was kind of young figuring this out, especially religion's role in our lives, which is maybe why I took on the attitude that God, to me, was a fraud. So, at a very young age, I stopped going to Church altogether. My thoughts leaned more toward everything being about big organizations, like the Church, our politicians, and the media being about entitlements, and believing they were our saviors and the ones that somehow knew what was best for us. I did have one thing going for me! I did experience seeing spirits, especially while I was in bed at night.

It began when I was about eight years old, and when going to bed, and after shutting my eyes, I would see spirits appear before me. At first, I was puzzled and somewhat frightened because what I saw was their shoulders on up to their faces and head. Nonetheless, it wasn't long before I found myself speaking to them without fear. Of course, once I did release my fear, I couldn't wait until bedtime just to see and talk with them again.

Being only eight years old at the time, today, I cannot remember most of what was said to me or me to them. However, I do remember when I was about ten, I found these spirits being very gentle when it came to framing themselves as to what they wanted me to see and hear. However, one night, it happened while lying in bed staring at them, and how I found myself speaking with two spirits and how they decided to tell me their names. And that was when I first learned they were Jesus and Mother Mary.

It was not long after that they both spoke of the name "Peter." Of course, hearing the name did not mean anything to me at that time, other than Peter being a disciple of Jesus. Nonetheless, all these communications with Jesus, Mother Mary, and other spirits suddenly stopped; it was as if someone turned off a switch. I remember feeling weird because I did not understand this sudden disappearance and why I did not see and hear from them anymore. I even remember as a ten-year-old, thinking to myself that maybe if I went back to Church on Sunday, they would come back and talk to me.

So, I decided to go to Church for a while. However, they still did not show themselves to me, so soon after, I stopped going to Church altogether. As I said, it puzzled me when I first saw them, and it puzzled me, even more, when it stopped. Anyway, I just let it go and went on with my life.

During my high school years, I still was not much of a student when it came to academics. However, I skated through High School with grades good enough to graduate at the age of seventeen. I guess I just did not have the passion and the appetite for school in those days. It was as if I felt burned out, even though we are speaking of only twelve years of schooling. Of course, I learned later that I had many lifetimes dealing with higher education, which was why I felt burned out during my high school years.

During my years of growing up going to school, especially eighth grade and below, my personality gravitated toward shyness, even though I did not show it on the outside too much. I was so afraid to speak with those in authority, such as priests, police, teachers, and all those of higher importance than myself. It feels weird to me saying this today because I got over those feelings many years ago.

However, I do remember thinking back about why I was afraid of people in those professions. I even remember being especially afraid of God, priests, and nuns. In fact, this fear of God and those of the cloth in my youth was more threatening than teachers, police, the rich, and the educated. It was as if I was trying to hide from them, which is why I never did like to talk or be around priests or nuns. I even hated to say the word "God." It was like I did not want God, priest, or nuns to find me. Of course, today, I know the feelings came from running from my true identity, as I will explain later in the book.

Aside from being afraid of God, priests, nuns, and those of authority, I remember feeling very uncomfortable with my everyday use of words, worried about not saying the right words; therefore, I lacked a lot of confidence in myself, which may explain why I was shy in my early years. Fortunately, things did change, and it all began after I graduated from High School. But before I get into that subject, let's move on with my education.

From eighth grade to when I graduated at seventeen, I worked in many places to earn money because my parents were not wealthy. If we needed to buy things for ourselves or have spending money growing up, we kids had to earn it ourselves. I was about thirteen years old when I began to work for farmers picking rocks in preparing the ground for planting potatoes and then later in the fall, picking the potatoes. From there, I worked in the potato barns packing and shipping potatoes.

Then I worked at rail depots working inside the train cars pushing sugar cane onto belts that brought the cane into the plant for processing. And then, in late summers, I would work at and with pea viners harvesting peas. I also worked at a grand hotel, washing dishes through high school. Back in those days, many kids took on many odd jobs to earn money for clothes and such.

Anyway, after I graduated from High School, I found myself having to sign up for selective service as this was the law and the system back then for drafting young men out of high school to fill the ranks of the U. S. Army.

I remember the government would do lottery picking of the names to serve in Vietnam, and many of my classmates got their lottery letters to go off to fight. But, for me, I never received one. Of course, I always wondered why! However, it wasn't until I was nineteen years old, two years after signing up for selective service, I had to go back to the selective service board to update my records to show that I was married with having a child on the way.

You see, if anyone's status changed from the time they first signed up at seventeen, like getting married and the wife is pregnant, you had to go back to the selective service board to update your files. So, when I did, and after the board looked into their files trying to find my selective service records, they confronted me about being sure I signed up at seventeen because they could not find my records. Luckily, when I signed up at seventeen, they gave me a selective service card showing compliance with the law. And once the selective service board looked at my card, realizing I had good evidence, they again searched for my records. After a while looking for them, they finally found them misfiled.

This explained why I never received my lottery letter to go and take a physical to be drafted into the Army. Once everything was cleared up, they then updated my records, giving me a class code stating that I was married and having a child on the way. Thus, deferring me from having to be drafted into the Army. Of course, today, I do not look at this as a coincidence, but as it was meant for me in this lifetime not to fight in any army.

It was about three years after graduation working as a laborer, when I came up with the idea to become a business owner. But, before becoming a successful businessman, it took many years of hard work to get there. For example, starting in late 1967, I found a job as an automotive parts runner working for a company having vehicle parts contracts with the U.S. Air Force. It was a time when I had an overwhelming passion for studying vehicle parts manuals that took me by surprise as it became the key that triggered within me the confidence and the courage to become a store manager.

Due to this confidence, it later gave me the passion for entering into the automotive parts business. Thus, in 1971, along with a good understanding of government contracts, I gathered up the courage to work something out where I could open up an automotive parts store as an owner to bid on Air Force contracts. However, because of very trying times, three and half years later, the company and I personally went bankrupt. The ordeal of not making it and filing bankrupt devastated my family and me because we lost everything of material value, even the house trailer we lived in at the time.

So, there I was at the age of twenty-three, and I lost all that I gained materially, along with losing my confidence, believing that I was not smart or educated enough to run a business. Of course, feeling down and depressed, it caused me to automatically, like a robot, think about God, the Church, and my fear of it all once again. So, that is when I began to pray as hard as I could, asking God to forgive me for not attending his Church.

Chapter 3

LIFE AFTER BANKRUPTCY

With my fear of God and the Church at this time, I always wondered if there was something wrong with me. After all, my thoughts and beliefs were not the same as my parents, grandparents, and siblings when it came to God and religion. And with the ordeal of my bankruptcies (business and personal), I felt foolish, embarrassed, and that I let my wife and family down. It was with these feelings that conditioned me to outright plead my case to God. Even my thoughts went toward attending Church again, believing if God saw me there, it would show my sincerity for redemption.

Of course, after praying and praying, night and day, for weeks and weeks, pleading and begging God for his help and forgiveness, and with receiving no answer, I felt that I was not important enough for God to answer. Therefore, I became very disappointed in myself and with God! I even convinced myself that this praying to God was not for me. That is when I mentioned to myself, "Why should I pray to God just because I failed in business, filed bankruptcy, and did not attend his church?" And because of the foregoing statement, you can say that it was right during my darkest hour when an overwhelming feeling came over me.

It was like feeling someone invisible around me, reaching out and whispering in my ear, saying, *"Why would God want you to fear him and think that he is mad because of not attending his Church? Don't you think that this would make God changeable, inconsistent, and confusing when it comes to his love?"* Hence, after hearing this in my ear, my thoughts shifted toward outright releasing God and religion from my life, or at least until I could do some research on him.

I thought that if God sent his only son, Jesus, to walk with us here on earth over two thousand years ago to teach us about unconditional love, not to judge, have compassion, and love thy neighbor as thyself, then wouldn't that make Jesus' teachings the opposite of God's teachings according to the Bible? Even at Jesus' death on the cross, he said, "Father, forgive them, for they know not what they do." (Luke 23:34)

It seemed, even in my darkest hour, all that the Church could do for me was perform rituals and ceremonies about a God that was very demanding, jealous, and revengeful, let alone inconsistent with his love. In fact, God's Son, Jesus, seemed to have more common sense and compassion than God himself. And since I did not understand this type of conditional principles coming from a God that requires worshipping or else, I kept with what I felt was right for me.

However, what I did not know at the time was that something was beginning to show some movement on my behalf, and it was when I completely ran out of money three days before payday, leaving my wife without any money to buy food and milk for the children. It happened while I was at work when my wife turned over our last few dollars to a neighbor that needed it more than we did. I guess maybe her heart was right in doing this! Because, within that same day, my wife won a twenty-dollar drawing at a local food store where she bought milk a few days before giving our last dollar to our neighbor.

Not only that, to our surprise, the very next day, my wife again won another twenty-dollar drawing at the same food store, giving us forty dollars, two days before payday. And, in 1975, forty dollars bought a lot of food. And, to top it all off, I was lying in bed late that same night of the second twenty-dollar drawing, looking up at the ceiling, trying to go to sleep; and, out of nowhere, I became aware of some distortion taking place with the ceiling.

Being captivated by what I saw, I watched the darkness of my bedroom and ceiling give way to the brightness of the night sky and how it was filled with glittering stars. I even turned to my wife lying next to me, wanting her to observe what I was seeing. However, she was asleep, so I turned my head back to staring at the glittering stars as if the roof of our bedroom was transparent. Then all of a sudden, I saw three Franciscan Monks emerge from the darkness of our bedroom. And once I became aware of them, they began to walk toward me, and then they stopped near the foot of our bed, standing shoulder to shoulder, gazing at me.

That is when I noticed their clothing was of traditional brown robes that Franciscans wear. The next thing I noticed, one of the Monks began to move closer to me, and at the same time, he removed his brown hood off his head. That is when I saw his grayish hair and his smiling face. And, as I laid in bed gazing at him, he began to speak to me, saying, *"Hello Terry, how are you doing?"* Of course, my reply was, "I am fine," even though I was not fine at the time. Then the Monk spoke to me again, saying, *"Terry, you were with us in another lifetime. And now, in this lifetime, it is meant for you to know the truth."* That is when I said, "Then what is the truth?"

The Monk smiled at me and walked backward toward his fellow Monks that were still standing at the foot of our bed. Then as fast as they appeared, they disappeared! A few days later, my thoughts moved towards reading the Bible since the two events of winning the food lottery and the Monk's visit were so uplifting, so maybe I should be reading the Bible. So, while still recovering from bankruptcy, I read the Bible cover to cover. Once I was finished, I had the incredible urge to go back to the beginning of Genesis and reread it as the desire was powerful.

That is when, for the very first time in my life, I started to have feelings about writing a book about Genesis. But the moment I formulated this desired thought in my mind, I remember thinking that I could not do that because I was not a writer. However, after that thought, I felt a compelling energy force move throughout my entire body. And that is when I heard a voice beyond the physical veil, telling me, *"Write a book about Genesis; learn to understand the wisdom of the book and then write what you feel is the interpretation of that wisdom."*

So, in late 1970, I did study Genesis, chapter by chapter, verse by verse, and that is when I began to notice a hidden message behind the literal words, even how the verses of the Bible were laid out in each chapter. However, when I studied Genesis in early 1975, I found myself very conflicted with my passion to get back into business. So, I pushed aside what I heard from the Monks and went back to focusing on getting back into my own business. When I did, I found myself back in business only eight months after my bankruptcy in early 1975.

Of course, back then, I did not have the financial backing to open a second time because of my bankruptcy; thus, leaving me completely broke. What I did have was the experience and knowledge about how the automotive parts industry worked. I also knew how to bid and win government contracts. So, I acquired a new partner that had some funds while I had the experience. With six thousand dollars that my new partner provided, we both managed to bid on my previous company's bankrupt inventory the courts held in escrow, and we won the bid. This then set us up to open a vehicle parts store outside of Loring AFB in Maine.

Because of my knowledge of the automotive parts industry, I then took the inventory and visited a well-known automotive parts distribution center in Bangor, Maine. And that is when I had them turn this inventory of the courts into a mixture of automotive parts that equaled in value of twenty-five thousand dollars. That was just enough in 1975 to open up a vehicle parts store outside of Loring AFB. Then a few months later, I bid on and won the vehicle parts bid at Loring AFB. From there, we won over twenty-six U.S. Air Force contracts throughout the continental United States, selling vehicle parts to the military.

When I went into this new partnership in 1975, and after my failure with my first company and learning not what to do, I believed that I had a partner of such spiritual integrity and trust that the thought of him betraying me never entered my mind. However, after eighteen years (1975-1993) working with him, I was kicked out of my own company because of failing to have a signed agreement with him. I felt like the rug was completely pulled out from beneath me, making me feel stupid, weak, and most of all, very betrayed.

I was so devastated by my partner's actions that I began to think about my first failure in 1975. I felt naive, and my thoughts were about how could God abandon me without any warning. I even remember justifying that thought because of my lack of miracles and how I disregarded the Monk's message about writing a book on the Bible's Genesis. It was a time in my life where all self-doubt came flowing in because there I was in 1993 again feeling all this fear toward God, and with such anxiety and dismay that I thought for sure, I was doomed.

Because of this fear of God, I found myself again praying to Him and the monks I saw in 1975. However, as I began to pray, a fantastic thing happened. I felt an overwhelming energy around me, where my thoughts moved toward the quieting of my mind, not to pray, just do deep breathing. So, after blaming myself for being stupid and allowing my mind to put me down as a failure, I began to sit still and take deep breaths.

At first, it was only a few minutes a day; then, I finally worked up to about thirty minutes a day. And yes, while I was doing this deep breathing, I remember how my mind continued to put me down for several months until, suddenly, and without warning, I noticed my mind was beginning to quiet down. That is when I felt my emotions on a conscious level and how out of balance I had become.

Yes, failing twice in business and losing my income can be very upsetting and to the point of feeling angry, clumsy, foolish, and very frustrated. Of course, what hurt the most was that I believed that I failed my family for the second time. However, instead of fighting off those feelings, I found myself allowing my emotional pain to come into my heart and consciousness and then breathe them in and out. And then finally, letting them go!

Then one day, after doing some deep breathing, out of nowhere, I began to feel someone speaking to me from beyond the physical veil. When I first felt this spirit energy attuning with me, I suspected my mind was visualizing it because of how I felt. Yet, despite what my mind judged it to be, I could feel the sincerity of someone speaking to me from beyond the physical veil.

At first, I thought of the Monks back in 1975. Then I had a feeling that it was not coming from my mind at all. It was a deep feeling that

I somehow knew, and what I was hearing was not coming from this physical world because I could hear a message coming through to my consciousness as if it was telepathically being downloaded. And what I heard as a message was amazing!

"It was not about your business, a signed agreement, family, education, where you were born, your intellect, or your failures, or even about God or Spirit. It was about the wisdom that you had learned from every experience and every encounter that you have had with yourself, with your past lifetimes, and with others in this lifetime." After hearing this message from beyond the physical veil, I then learned to trust only in what I was feeling coming from within and leaving the outside world to a God of judgment and conditional principles.

That is when I finally allowed myself to let go of all fear of God and his Church. I learned that my fear of God in my early years came from many lifetimes knowing that this God of the Bible was a false God and how I always worked in those lifetimes in disclosing him as a fraud that resulted in me getting persecuted and killed. Then in that same breathing session, and after the first downloaded message, I heard a new message, telling me:

"Along your path of many lifetimes contains the wisdom of your experiences, and when you place 'all that you are' as only in this lifetime because of those beliefs, your upbringing, and who you think you are, then you cannot bring forth the wisdom of those experiences to your outer consciousness. And because of it, you have been separated from your higher soul self and all the wisdom it possesses. Therefore, being aware of 'who you truly are' is more important than all the treasures, education, and power in the world."

From my deep breathing, and then letting go of this God of the Bible because of not understanding his dualistic principles, I reconnected with my higher "I AM" Christ consciousness, and at the same time, with many well-known Ascended Masters that are mentioned in the Bible, including Jesus, Mother Mary, Lord Melchizedek, and Mary Magdalene, just to mention a few. And what was said to me next by these angelic beings from beyond the physical veil was more than amazing.

Their message to me was that they did not care about any signed agreement, my intellect, money, success, fame, fear of God or me loving God, or my religious views; all that they wanted for me to do was to become "aware" of who I truly am as a divine being because I am not who I believe I am. It was immediately after I received these first two messages that I again heard the words downloaded to my consciousness:

"Once you understand this, then all of those things and more will come to you automatically anyway because you would be "aware" of who you are as a God and a Christ also, therefore drawing toward you all that comes with the knowing of who you truly are."

Chapter 4

MY NEXT ADVENTURE

After these wonderful messages given to me from the Ascended Masters, there I was, in the fall of 1993, a few months after being kicked out of my own company, I again found a way to get back in business for the third time. But this time, I used my name, as I identified my company as "Newbegin Enterprises Inc.," short for NEI. Oddly, because my wife and I held a small savings this time around, I did not have to file bankruptcy. With my brother-in-law's help, this allowed me to borrow money from a bank to open the business.

At first, I worked out of the basement of my home until the spring of 1994. Shortly after, I made enough profits to move into a leased building in Somerset, Pennsylvania. And, from April 1994 to December 1994, my sales volume reached about $94,000 respectively. Today, the year 2020, my annual business sales have reached about twenty-seven million, and I have written several books based on the wisdom found behind the biblical text. And now, with Jesus, Lord Melchezidek, and the Ascended Masters at my side channeling through me, I bring you a new kind of book that is filled with messages of wisdom to help those that are ready to awaken to the fifth-dimensional consciousness.

However, before diving into these channeled messages, I would like to reflect back on my former partner of eighteen years. He always showed himself as a very spiritual and trusting person at the beginning of our business relationship in 1975. But later, in 2000, he found himself losing the very company we started together in 1993, as he lost everything. And even though things did not turn out for him, I still stuck to trusting myself and the people around me. I took on a philosophy that my experiences with Spirit would help me learn to trust my intuitive feelings more than my mind, intellect, and emotions.

I say this because of channeling the ascended masters and how they have helped me understand that there is no such thing as sin, death, judgment, or evil. They have taught me that everything is only as spirit, consciousness, and experiencing, which is why I could forgive my former partner and myself without any attachments. However, from what I had experienced so far about my business adventures, you would think that everything from then on would evolve into a happy, ever after scenario. But, as many of you know, life can sometimes be deceiving.

Because of losing sight of my purpose, it happened to me again, for the third time. And it left me in such confusion that I began to question everything about my choices, including my understanding of what I was receiving from beyond the physical veil from the ascended masters. After my first business failure, I used the excuse of fearing God, the Church, feeling unworthy, where I was born, and not intellectual or educated enough to run a business. And, as a result, I ended up using my emotions as an excuse this time around.

One would think that after all of what I had experienced concerning the business world, I would become enlightened enough to control my emotions. But, what I forgot, and this can sneak up on anyone, is that your soul will undoubtedly take you out of your comfort zone without you even realizing it.

So, from what I have learned about God, Christ, and Spirit in the last thirty years or so, I can say this! Even if you attend Church regularly or belong to a particular religion, and that you are devoted to your preacher and political party, you too, will one day (either in this lifetime or the next) come to a point in life where you will change your thinking, because you, like me, will finally give up and let this God of the Bible and his dualistic laws of duality, and your affiliations (prayers) to your preacher, Church, sin, and political party, go. Why? Because they are all lies!

Please forgive me, as I will speak more on this later in the book. But for now, back to my ordeal with the business world.

Back in September 2000, I decided to move my new company from Pennsylvania to Eastern Tennessee. And during the process, I hired an excellent "IT Computer Programmer," one who knew computer code very well. And with my eldest son's help, we decided to develop an electronic web-based e-procurement system to buy and sell parts to the military. And, after its completion, the system became very popular with the U.S. Air Force. So much so that NEI's company's annual sales moved past three million dollars within the first two years of our move to Tennessee.

Because of the company's success with this e-procurement system, we decided to have our "IT Programmer" develop a new e-procurement system to accommodate city and state governments as well to reduce their cost as it did for the U.S. Air Force. After a few weeks of working with the new system, we found a city to test it for six months, and their savings reached about ten percent. However, to market this new system, I knew that I had to hire a very skillful marketer. So, before hiring this person, I decided to create an LLC (Limited Liability Company) to protect myself personally, the company (NEI), and its sales to the U.S. Air Force.

Then it came to financing this LLC venture! The question was, how was I going to finance the project? So, I decided to use the profits from NEI to support this LLC venture. The funding was a loan from NEI to the LLC, and it was used to cover the expenses for this skillful marketer to go out and sell this new idea to cities and states until the LLC could make enough to survive on its own.

This decision proved to be a bad and unpleasant one on my part because once everything was in place, including the funding, I hired a highly-educated individual whose credentials suggested that he was the expert needed in marketing such a system. This person was well known throughout some large companies and was very skilled in the art of persuasion, which is why I believed he was the perfect individual to market this new system. After all, the e-procurement system that NEI's IT department built for the U.S. Air Force proved very profitable and cost-saving to the Air Force.

I even vetted this person myself, as he again was well known by large companies, and they hired him on a part-time basis to market their products throughout the world. Therefore, I thought, if he was good enough for them, then he was good enough to market this city and state e-procurement system for the LLC. However, the only way I could hire this individual was to offer him part ownership in the LLC.

Believing that I had everything in place to launch this new city and state e-procurement system, I offered to give away forty-nine percent of the LLC to a few individuals that I felt would help get it off the ground. I would retain fifty-one percent to keep control since I was funding it. I gave twenty percent to this highly skilled and persuasive person and the other twenty-nine percent to other highly educated people. And from my perspective, I believed I assembled the right people to get this new city and state e-procurement system out in the market. I was even somewhat proud of myself.

Of course, we all agreed to launch this new system in Tennessee since NEI was already located there. I also managed to acquire a former mayor, a former city manager, and a former city attorney to assist us with what I believed would be the best-qualified team put together to launch the e-procurement system. But, to make a long story short, this highly persuasive person, after a few years of marketing the system with his twenty-percent ownership, ended up turning my life upside down.

I could not believe that I found myself drawn into his web of lies and fabricated stories with not feeling this from a spiritual level. It was as if I had never connected to Spirit before hiring this charlatan and artificial personality. It took me a bit over three years to learn that he was nothing more than an impostor registering himself as someone in the know. What a dummy I thought I was for hiring him.

Not only did I give this impostor twenty percent of the LLC, but I also provided him with thousands of dollars to market the system, with having no results. It took me some time to realize that all he was doing was spending NEI profits. Thus, in the end, I failed to see and feel the deceit that came from this man, but I did feel it financially. Because of his persuasive and deceptive nature, I set myself up to where I nearly lost NEI in 2004.

It was a time when I found NEI deep in the red for the first time since its inception in 1993. With NEI, I was actually out of funds and owing vendors a lot of money. I was actually hanging on with a very thin thread. Therefore, once again, my thoughts went back to God and the Church, my education, and maybe I was just not smart enough to run a business.

Because of my naivety and passion for business, my focus on success was essentially controlled by my emotions, and therefore my choices. I even held back raises to NEI employees because the profits were used for the LLC venture, leaving nothing extra for them. Not understanding this at the time made it unfair to the employees who worked hard for NEI. It was as if I had not learned from my past failures and my spirit communications with the Monks in 1975.

Even with the encounters of Jesus and Mother Mary at a very young age, it did not seem to shed any light on what I was doing until I was faced with the idea of failing again for the third time. However, this time I felt that I was doomed for sure. Therefore, I went back to praying again! Yet, this time I did not pray to God. I found myself appealing to the three Monks that had visited me back in 1975.

Then one evening, after going to bed and doing some extensive pleading to the Monks, a huge rustic, brownish door appeared right in front of me. It seemed to be made of wood. But, as I stared at this massive wooden door, I saw three large metal straps and hinges that were about three inches wide that went across the top, middle, and bottom of the door. As I looked at this huge door, I noticed no door handle or any combination sequence to open the door.

Of course, puzzled by this, the door suddenly began to open on its own. And as the door slowly opened, I noticed how robust this wooden door was, as it looked at least two-to-three feet thick. It was like I was looking at a thick bank vault. And as this massive door opened wider and wider, I saw eight spirits sitting around a wooden picnic table. There were four spirits on one side of the table and four on the other side, sitting there facing each other. And once the heavy-looking door was wide open, I went from lying in bed to standing in the doorway of this vault-looking door.

These eight spirits then turned and looked at me while I was standing there looking at them. It was then that I seemed to feel their energy, clarifying what I saw before my eyes. Then one of them said to me: "*Welcome to the wisdom of the Bible.*" Once this was said, these eight spirits began to introduce themselves to me. From one side of the picnic table, the first to introduce himself was Jesus, then Mother Mary, then Mary Magdalene, then Tobias, also known as Tobit in the Old Testament.

On the other side of the picnic table, Lord Melchizedek was the first to speak to me, as he stated that he would be the group leader for my writings. Then the next Spirit introduced himself as Kuthumi Lal Singh, known as Saint Frances of Assai. Then Adamus Saint Germain, known in the Old Testament as Samuel. Then the eighth Spirit introduced himself as Moses, the author of Genesis.

After the introductions, Lord Melchizedek beckoned me to enter the room. So, confused a bit, I moved forward, crossing the threshold of the vault looking door, finding myself in the room or the dimension with these well-known Masters. Then Lord Melchizedek, the group leader, explained that they were there to help me with the Bible's interpretations, as they are experts when it comes to the Bible, Christ, Consciousness, and God.

Lord Melchizedek also informed me that *"I was a person that always enjoyed being on the front line when it came to matters of the Divine; and that I was a priest under the order of Melchizedek."* And after Lord Melchizedek's words found my ears, and with him smiling, he informed me that I do not have to do this work only if I choose to do so.

After experiencing these Ascended Masters, I then found myself back in bed, and all that I saw was beginning to fade away. Once I became aware of my surroundings again, I realized that these honorable Ascended Masters said nothing about my business situation. After a few months past in seeing these Masters, I thought that I was destined to lose my business for the third time with nothing being done about NEI's financial condition.

However, one morning while lying in bed about ready to get up, and around seven o'clock, the year 2004, I became overwhelmed as Jesus manifested himself before me in material form. Jesus looked at me and then shared a message, telling me that *"Everything with my business situation would be fine."* Then as quickly as Jesus appeared and gave me the message, he dissipated back into non-physical form. And yet, as I rose from the bed and walked into the bathroom to shower, still being very overwhelmed in seeing Jesus in the physical, I could feel Jesus' presents, as he stayed around and talked with me in non-physical form for a few minutes more before he finally departed.

Note: Not that I believe that I am different or special because of Jesus manifesting himself in the flesh before me. It is that everyone is special in the eyes of Jesus. Jesus' remarks to me were that *"Anyone can experience Christ!"* And that *"He is available to anyone that seeks their own "I AM" sovereignty as a divine being and not as someone that is looking to be saved."*

After my encounter with Jesus, I then got ready and left for work. Within an hour of being at work, I gathered all those that were part of the LLC, and that is when I told them that I was closing it down. And since I owned fifty-one percent of the LLC, I was legally allowed to do so. And yes, I heard plenty of protest, threats, and warnings about closing it down. But it did not matter because what I said to them next was that they were all fired. I told them that I would take full responsibility for the losses and dissolve the LLC with the hope of getting NEI up and running solvent again.

I also mentioned to the investors who put money into the LLC that I would write a promissory note to pay them back with interest. I said that the reason I was dissolving the LLC was that my focus is going back to NEI, where it belonged. And after doing this, I never before felt so liberated.

After thirty-three years of struggling with the ups and downs of business (1971-2004), I remember thinking and feeling clear of any guilt, fear, and shame. It was as if I knew I could finally let go of my fears and doubts about being good enough to run a business even though I was broke. In fact, by experiencing Jesus in my bedroom, I remember how I felt his presence and how I released all appearances of fear. That was when I decided to take the Ascended Masters offer and write as many books as they would like for me to write.

Therefore, back in 2004, I ultimately came into trusting myself to be the perfect person to plan, make decisions, and choose my own direction when it came to the business. It was also when I began to communicate with Spirit to do my writings because of having a better understanding of my business and them. The timing was perfect! After all, I released all fear of losing my company, fearing God, fearing the Devil, fearing Christ, Sin, and feeling guilty because I did not adhere to the Monks Genesis writings back in 1975.

It was from that moment in consciousness, in 2004, when I experienced Jesus manifesting before me, and when I began to see a new world of non-judgment, non-duality, complete compassion, who God and Christ are, and the freedom of being sovereign. From that moment in my awakening back in 2004 and to what the Monks message was to me back in 1975, my business did a complete turnaround to where I paid off all business debts, including those investors that I had promissory notes.

And not only that, I have written several books on what Jesus and the Ascended Masters regard as books filled with wisdom and certainty. Thus, informing those that are willing and ready to open up to the wisdom of their "Oversoul." It was from my visit with the Monks in 1975 to my visit with Jesus and the Ascended Masters in 2004 that I had finally learned the meaning of what the Monks meant when they said, *"It was meant for me to learn the real truth in this lifetime."*

What better way to learn this "truth" than for me to be born a Catholic, not holding the same beliefs as my parents and siblings, and meeting and working with people with a personality nature that challenged me to my very core. From going into business three times and experiencing firsthand the manipulation of truth, seeing how persuasion and deception work, to where I was born, to my visitations from the Monks, to seeing Jesus materialize in front of me, I had to experience the untruths, the deceptions, the lies, and cover-ups, and all that was hidden within my own soul memories, including this false God of the Bible, before I could come into the realization of the "real truth" that the Monks mentioned in 1975.

All of it eventually led to my awakening in this lifetime as a Christ in my own right. In other words, to recognize not only the Church's dark forces and their teaching of this false God of the Bible, one must first learn the true identity of "who you believe you are" before recognizing these dark-minded humans that have been stealing your energy for a very long time. And it can only come from within yourself and not outside of yourself.

We all have forgotten that "we are not who we believe we are," because being aware of 'who we truly are' is more important than who we believe we are when it comes to an understanding of yourself, God, Christ, your human existence, where you come from, who created you, and your purpose on earth. Thus, it is time for you to awaken to "Who you are, not who you believe you are."

Chapter 5

REINCARNATION

In 2013, I had a channeling session with a friend in Colorado who is a fantastic channeler. And in that session, Lord Melchezidek made a special appearance where he presented to her a group of messages that he wanted me to hear. And yes, this is the same Lord Melchezidek that helped Abraham back in the day of Sodom and Gomorrah. What was interesting about this channeling was what happened right after Lord Melchezidek's messages. Because, from out of nowhere, he mentioned to me that someone I know wants to speak with me.

Suddenly, a brief silence came over the channeler herself as she was making the transition from Lord Melchezidek to channeling this distinctive angelic messenger. Then from the mouth of the channeler, Lord Christ Jesus began to speak with me. Talk about being surprised! I was completely in disbelief, but as Jesus spoke to me, the more I realized that I was speaking to someone extraordinary and how it was such an honor to hear his message to me.

After Jesus' greetings, along with still feeling dumbfounded and confused at the same time, Jesus began his message to me and how it was about a past lifetime that I had with him when I was the Son of Jonah. Of course, first hearing this come from Jesus, my thoughts went to, "I had a lifetime with Jesus, and who is Jonah?"

After the initial shock, Jesus then gave me more messages and then closed out the channeling by giving us, the channeler and myself, many blessings. Then it hit me after Jesus' departure that Jesus did not clarify who the Son of Jonah was, as he seemed to have left that part up to me to find out for myself. Of course, once the channeler was back to herself, I then asked her if she knew who the Son of Jonah was. That was when she informed me that the Son of Jonah was Simon Peter and that Jonah was his father.

Now, when the channeler said this to me, I automatically responded to her, "Do you mean the Jonah from the Bible?" She said yes, Jonah and Simon Peter were Father and Son! (I want to note here that when Jesus spoke to me, it was with such love and gentleness.)

After hearing this, the first thing I did when I returned to my office was that I picked up the Bible and looked up the "Son of Jonah." And, to my surprise, it was indeed Simon Peter! And yes, the very same Simon Peter that was Jesus' disciple over two thousand years ago. And after allowing this information to sink in, my thoughts moved quickly to, "Maybe the channeler and I misinterpreted Jesus' message."

However, after listening to the recording and reflecting on Jesus' message, a feeling of clarification began to set in because when I saw Jesus and Mother Mary in my youth when they spoke the name Peter to me in my bedroom, it kind of fit the narrative. It was not that "Peter's" name came into my mind every day growing up, but his name, as a disciple, sure impacted me while growing up because down deep within my soul, the message just felt right to me.

Of course, I was not always aware of having a lifetime as Simon Peter or even who I was before and after Peter. However, as I mentioned before, I remember when I was ten years old, I would see Mother Mary and Jesus in my bedroom, speaking the name Peter to me just about every time I saw them. And now, I wondered why Jesus chose that particular time (2013) in my life to mention that I had a lifetime with him as Simon Peter. Today, after thinking about it, I understand why Jesus gave me the message on that day.

It just would not have worked before that particular channeling in 2013. I would not have been ready to hear it before that time. Jesus waited until the perfect time for me to be ready, spiritually, physically, mentally, and emotionally. And his underlying message was that I am still his disciple even though I carry a different name and body in this lifetime.

In Matthew 16:17-19: *"Blessed are you, Simon Barjona,* meaning Son of Jonah, *because flesh and blood did not reveal this to you, but my father in heaven; And, I also say to you that you are Peter, and upon this rock I will build my church and the gates of Hades will not overpower it; I will give you the keys of the kingdom of heaven."*

"Giving Simon Peter the keys to the kingdom of heaven" has nothing to do with what Peter did back in the time of Jesus. It has the meaning of Jesus reminding me in this lifetime, as Terry, that I am still his disciple and I still have the keys to the kingdom (higher consciousness) in bringing forth truth.

Therefore, not only do I have the wisdom of the Christ consciousness within me, I also have the eternal authority to enter into multidimensional realms, from higher to lower, and lower to higher, in presenting to those who have the eyes to see and the ears to hear the truth about "you are not who you believe you are." And as it was for me during the lifetime as Simon Peter, it is for me in this lifetime, as Terry, to announce the harvesting of those souls that are ready to ascend to a fifth-dimensional consciousness frequency that Jesus spoke about over two thousand years ago.

In other words, I am here, as a disciple of Christ once again in this lifetime, to help those that are ready to be harvested, like in a Rapture, but with a Rapture having the meaning of you coming out of your sleep state (or mind control) and moving into the fifth dimension of being sovereign. And as some may know, Simon Barjona is another term for the Son of John and the Son of Jonah, as they are the same person. And further insight into this connection can be found in Revelation 6:7-8, as it mentions the fourth seal and the pale green horse, and its rider was named Death, and Hades accompanied him.

The name "Hades" in Hebrew means "Sheol," which primarily refers to death or asleep or unaware of oneself and one's purpose. This means "Hades" is a state of consciousness in which the dead has a meaning of not being aware of one's "I AM" Christ eternal Godship where one is equal to and not less than God himself because one is

God, Christ, and the Goddess. Therefore, people are alive and walking around on earth but very much asleep (dead) to whom they truly are at their core consciousness, all because of mind control done by the media, the world's churches, and our politicians.

Therefore, Jesus' message is that I am still his disciple, even though I am in a new time setting and physical body. In other words, the death (forgetfulness) of Simon Peter did not overpower me to who "I AM" today because Christ has given me the "key to my soul memories" where I can enter into the wisdom of "all that I am" as a Christ also (the kingdom of heaven) and then pass that wisdom and truth on to others who would listen.

And as the fourth seal in Revelation's 6:7-8 has nothing to do with Jesus, Satan, God, or Death, the wisdom behind the verses is for those that are ready to "remember" that they are the ones that created the belief in "sin." We believe in sin because of feeling guilty about what we have created in the realm of using energy, both physically and non-physically, throughout our many lifetimes.

And with it, many of us carry within our soul a lot of guilt, shame, and forgetfulness because of misusing energy, not because of sin. Sin is just a name we gave it because of the misuse of energy. Of course, it has been religions' dark forces, the media, and the world's governments (politicians) that have kept us asleep for many lifetimes as being a slave to them and a God that created us. Not only that, but we must worship some God outside of us, and for us to give all that we have to the application of life; otherwise, sin and punishment would be the price for our disobedience.

Therefore, the opening of the fourth seal in Revelation is about those individuals that are beginning to come to an awakening that there was never a reason to feel guilty about sinning because, in truth, there is no such thing as "sin." It is for us to know that there is only spirit consciousness, which is our true existence, and that of choosing, experiencing, and learning the wisdom behind our choices. Remember, consciousness is just consciousness and has nothing to do with a physical body other than giving it animation.

The voice coming from the "fourth living creature" in Revelation 6:7 is that of our mental level of consciousness (our mind) and how most of us today are beginning to remember and are now questioning not only our politicians, but also church teachings, such as in Satan, sin, and separation. Thus, the phrase "come forward" is actually about us souls, in our awakening, to open up to the mind and how it is limited to knowing the true Self, God, Spirit, and Christ.

The "pale green horse" represents one's soul growth patterns in what we have learned about ourselves journeying through many, many lifetime experiences. And just as the color "green" represents vegetation and soul growth, "sickly green" is an outgrowth of our physical Cain consciousness where we are very judgmental, full of jealousy, and that fear and our emotions have been the basis of our choices journeying through many lifetimes, all because of the belief in sin as being real.

The "rider" is the self or that of one's many physical Cain personalities (name and stories) journeying in and out of many incarnations, and each one of these ego personalities are still part of one's consciousness today. That is the reason why we experience pain, joy, illness, and sorrow here on earth. And, as we pass through the fire of justice (karma), our spirit (the Christ) is always with us as we journey through time and space, learning to take full responsibility for our creations.

As a Goddess and a Christ also, we know that we gave ourselves the gift of life, and all that we chose to experience, good and bad, was for soul growth and to learn wisdom. Thus, "Death and Hades" became our belief in sin and separation, as our own Christ consciousness gave them life as if they were real. Hades represents, lifetime after lifetime, how we buried and hid our appalling creations deep within our Oversoul memories, all because of not wanting to take responsibility for them.

This created within our consciousness a memory of a Devil/Satan to blame, as this Devil is just an outer reflection of what we refuse to acknowledge as our own dark creations. And since we deny these appalling acts (sins) that we chose in our many lifetimes, we then take on a belief in sin and a Devil to blame in order for us to move forward in consciousness.

It was and is because of this belief in sin; we all return to earth from near earth realms to play out our choices and actions over and over (karma) in many different physical bodies. This is also why it is easy to become mentally and emotionally controlled by the church, the media, our politicians, and others that do not have our best interest at hand. Even our own family members do not have our best interests. It comes down to where most of us would rather keep the belief in sin and that there is only one lifetime to live, and that a savior outside of us is going to come from out behind some cloud to save us instead of us awakening to one being responsible for whatever is happening in our lives.

Many people have asked me, because of my writings, was I born with the name "Newbegin, or did I change it to Newbegin?" With that question, my answer has always been; I was born with the name Newbegin, which is the name on my birth certificate. My first name Terry has a meaning, "the harvester," and is also known as a "reaper." And my last name, "Newbegin," is tied to the energy frequency about a "new beginning or awakening," an awakening for those who are ready to ascend to a higher frequency understanding of God, Christ, Satan, sin, and who they are.

As I have had many channeled conversations with Jesus since 2013 on the subject of Simon Peter, he had disclosed to me that when he (Jesus) was with us here on the earth, his many conversations with his disciples were about reincarnation. And this is why Jesus gave me this message about having an incarnation as Simon Peter. It was to help me expand my consciousness and open up to receiving the aspect of Simon Peter and other incarnational aspects about myself since Earth's beginning, and allow them to come into my consciousness as "one body of consciousness." You know, God is one! I AM ONE as a Christ also!

And as most know, the subject of reincarnation regarding Church teachings is described as blasphemy and offensive against God and the Church. Why is that? Since Jesus left over two thousand years ago, and after three hundred years of his death, the Churches around the world felt it was best not to teach the people about reincarnation because they were afraid of losing their control over the people's minds and actions. They felt it was best for them to be the go-between since they knew more about God and Jesus than we did about God's meaning when it came to reincarnation.

The church wanted to keep us in our minds so we would not seek Christ out as being our higher consciousness. By not teaching reincarnation, it gave religion the ability to program our minds into believing that we needed a savior outside of us to control our spiritual path instead of one being Christ. Thus, we fell right into their trap and gave them our power as a Christ and all the energy tied to it. This is why the name "Jesus" became a code word for religion when they say, "follow Jesus, worship Him, and allow Him to guide you," without realizing it subliminal for you to follow a religion.

This lie gave them the power to steal our soul, our money, our energy and to build them amazing structures to keep them living in luxury and entitlement while we ordinary folks stayed broke, suffered, and asleep (dead) to their mind control. This was evident when Jesus himself was placed on the cross for blasphemy when he taught the people about reincarnation, and that one was a Christ-God-Goddess also.

Of course, once the disciples of Jesus understood reincarnation and that everyone is a Christ, they began to teach it throughout the land. However, once the disciples began teaching reincarnation, and that one is a Christ also, as Jesus did, religion chose to work with the government authorities to stop these teachings. Jesus never denied reincarnation. In fact, he agreed to it, such as when he referred to John the Baptist as Elijah. If John the Baptist was not Elijah returning to earth during the time of Jesus, what would that imply about Jesus's legitimacy? (Matthew 17:10-13). It is evident that Jesus was speaking of the reincarnation of Elijah as John the Baptist.

When Jesus spoke to the Jews in the Temple of Jerusalem, he said, "Is it not written in your law, I say, you are gods?" (John 10:34). So, if you are God, then what is the reason for you to be here? It is for soul growth, experiencing, choosing, and reincarnation to play it all out to learn wisdom.

Scripture tells us that those who live by the sword will sooner or later be destroyed by the sword (Matthew 26:52) and that a man will reap only what he sows (Galatians 6:7). If this is not so, why does an innocent child contract a fatal disease or be held hostage for child abuse? Or, how about a very good loving and giving person contracting a fatal disease? That is because it is not about contracting some disease because of God deciding it was one's turn. It is about reincarnation and learning the wisdom of our choices, which is why we experience cause and effect.

In John 9:2-4, the "disciples asked Jesus whether a blind man had sinned or his parents that he had been born blind." Jesus's reply was, "It was so that the works of God may be made manifest in the blind man." What did Jesus mean by that? Jesus was speaking about the "law of cause and effect" being fulfilled, as it was the God within the blind man coming back to reap what he sowed in a past lifetime.

In many places, the Bible states that we reap what we sow, for the blind man could not have sown the seeds of his blindness in his present lifetime, for he was born blind. Therefore, he must have done so in a previous lifetime where the choice was made before he was born in the flesh in his present lifetime, and in that present lifetime, he reaped that choice. Just know that existence does not know how to become non-existent.

And, as Jesus stated in John 10:34, we are all gods. Then "I," as well as all of us, are part of "all" that is God, and therefore every member of it is the one, God. In other words, there is nothing outside of God because everything is an integral part of that oneness of God. This means that God is not a deity unto himself or some white man in charge of "all that is," including us humans, but is the makeup of all souled beings no matter what race or gender a soul takes up in a human body.

If anyone went out of existence, God would be incomplete, which is impossible. Therefore, God does not banish anyone to damnation because it would be like you banishing yourself or God banishing God. It wasn't until the Council of Constantinople, five hundred years after the death of Jesus, the reincarnation doctrine was openly taught by the new church at that time. Later, censorship was passed by the Council regarding the doctrine of rebirth even though that censorship was in direct opposition to the words of Jesus himself.

In effect, religion said that Jesus did not know enough to correct or condemn the belief in reincarnation. Thus, it proves that the intellect and those who feel they are above another, combined by mind control and ego, became the powerhouse over their own "I AM" Christ spirit. Therefore, man's mind becomes the Anti-Christ, and the ego becomes the beast, as in the Cain consciousness killing one's awareness (Abel) in knowing one is God and the Christ.

Incarnating into many physical bodies can also be found within the wisdom behind Genesis, Chapter 4:12, where it states a *"restless wanderer on the earth."* A "restless wanderer" is not only a human wandering around earth blinded by their own ego, but it also relates to us souls incarnating into many parallel physical bodies and a world playing with the belief that there is a God and a Satan outside of us trying to appear as good and evil.

Hence, as a God-Goddess, and a Christ also, we souled beings, by allowing our mind and ego consciousness to play opposite roles using many conflicting vibrational energy frequencies to learn "all that there is to know" about dense energy, is where we learn the wisdom to "who we truly are at our core essence." Just in the wisdom behind the word "wanderer" itself stands for reincarnation.

The wisdom behind the word "earth" itself is symbolic of us humans moving between differing vibrating energy frequencies and that of many physical bodies to learn the wisdom behind our choices by playing them out on earth. This way, in the end, we become a much wiser God than when we first left the Garden (Higher Consciousness).

And, when Cain said to the Lord in Genesis 4:13-14, *"My punishment is too great to bear since you have now banished me from the soil, and avoid your presence and become a restless wanderer on the earth, anyone could kill me at sight,"* is not about one's punishment that is too great to handle because of reincarnation. It is about a "restless wanderer" is not about the part of you that is God, Christ, and the Goddess having to experience flesh but is the part of you that is your ego-personality consciousness coming into the flesh and becoming a restless wanderer because of not believing you are God, the Christ, and the Goddess all rolled up as "one body of consciousness."

In fact, Cain represents the dark side of all of us that uses dual-energy for evil acts. In other words, Abel represents that side of the mind that reconnects us to a higher awareness where we come into a knowing that we are indeed God, Christ, and the Goddess. In contrast, Cain represents that side of us that works against itself for the betterment of gaining wisdom.

Therefore, the punishment (karma) one receives comes directly from one's own judgments, attitudes, and obsessions with one's strong belief in dual-energy, like good, evil, and that power is something real. This is why in a three-dimensional world, we are brainwashed and programmed into believing that God's followers are good and the Devil's followers are evil. And yet, both good and evil are all bound to the mind that is very much asleep to one's own Christ consciousness. Thus, even though many are asleep to it, we are a multi-dimensional consciousness riding the rails of having many belief systems and incarnations playing in the dark and in the light.

Jesus called it reincarnation and dimensions, and the Bible states it as "in my father's house there are many mansions or kingdoms." In the eyes of Cain, symbolic of our descended ego-personality here on earth rebelling against itself, is the consciousness part of us that fell from grace (Heaven).

And now, many of us have lowered our consciousness to a denser three-dimensional one that works out of an energy frequency that brings us great punishment because of believing in dual-energy, positive and negative, good and evil, as being real.

My friends, they are not real, and you in your physical state are not real. However, the magic is in rediscovering your Christ consciousness once you play out your journey within many lifetime ego consciousnesses (dimensions-Kingdoms), enduring the punishments you place on yourself because of your beliefs. Remember, belief systems are what create our truths, lies, and reality. This, in effect, allows us to become balanced in consciousness to where we become awakened to our own Christ consciousness.

Let's suppose one's descended ego-personality consciousness cannot learn to reconnect itself to one's higher awareness, symbolized by Abel, Cain's brother, to whom Cain had killed. In that case, one does not awaken to one's misguided beliefs about sin and duality and how they are not real. And yet, they feel real so as to experience one's choices. How can one's fallen ego-personality become one again with Christ if one keeps on denying the Christ within?

Once we understand the wisdom behind the challenging energies of opposing forces, namely positive and negative, and who God and

Satan are, we will move beyond what the ego's belief in power brings to us to work out in a lifetime. And, as a collective group, we all need to learn to challenge our belief systems when it comes to good and evil, right and wrong, sin, or we will remain in ignorance (darkness) forever. Through the belief in good and evil as being real keeps us faithfully devoted to the earth's dark forces.

Remember what Jesus said to Nicodemus in John 3:3, *"I say to you, no one can see the kingdom of God without being born from above."* Born from above is where we souls, at the beginning of our awareness of being Christ eons ago, is when our consciousness vibrated at a very high frequency. And in time, because of misunderstanding ourselves as a Christ, we, from the ego level, became restless wanderers creating multiple realities, names, stories, and physical bodies to help us grow in wisdom by experiencing our belief systems repeatedly until we learn the wisdom of the choice.

Cain, Genesis 4:15, being avenged sevenfold has nothing to do with anyone killing our ego personalities of many lifetimes. It is about us living in a physical body carrying an ego-personality consciousness of such ignorance to whom we are as God, Christ, and a Goddess that we become dead inside and outside leaving you vulnerable to the seven-fold mentioned in Genesis 4:15. In other words, this verse is symbolic of the "seven deadliest acts of our ego-consciousness" that you use as your belief systems that keep you locked into a mental and physical consciousness where you experience the seven deadliest acts (sins) without realizing it as if they are real. And these acts (or sins) are (i) sadness, (ii) anger, (iii) lust for power, (iv) envy, (v) pride, (vi) greed, and (vii) laziness.

It is with these "seven deadly acts of consciousness" that keep us as part of a three-dimensional physical reality without realizing that we are all part of the Spirit of One (God-Goddess). In other words, our Christ consciousness does not judge or punish us for our "choices or what we do as sins" because sin is an illusion and a lie to keep us as slaves to those that say God is outside of us and therefore must be worshipped and followed without question. It is about our descending biased ego-personality consciousness that perpetuated a belief by playing the judge and jury in what we chose to do in a particular lifetime.

However, we can stop our sowing and reaping and the incarnating by merely becoming awakened to the misinterpretation of who we are and who we are not at our core. And once this is understood from the fallen ego-personality aspect (three-dimensional world) and from the mind (the intellect), we would then be ready to ascend (like in a harvest) to a higher vibrational consciousness. For example, before and after my death as Simon Peter, I have incarnated on earth as a Warrior, a Monk, a Priest, a Rabbi, a Sheikh, a Shaman, and a Scholar. And now, I live upon this earth today as one awakened to my Christ consciousness.

Furthermore, with additional conversations with Jesus and the Masters, I have also learned about other incarnations, such as my existence in China's great civilization, along with Turkey, Israel, Egypt, Greece, and even during the Lemurian era, and that of the Atlantean era. I have had lifetimes with Abraham, Solomon, and David. I have held high positions and had great power in some of those lifetimes, but I was very fair and balanced with that power. I was even around during the American Civil War, as I lived in Washington, DC, as a politician.

And today, my light is exceptionally illuminating and commanding as my source of life and authority as a Christ also. And my objective today is to help others claim their own "I AM" Christ sovereignty, light, and wisdom over those that love to steal their power and the free will to choose. Because of my many incarnations as a Shepherd of the Church and as a disciple of Christ, I identify with the wisdom behind the Bible's scriptures and what it all means to get folks awakened to those that love to keep you asleep to steal your energy.

Not only was I a Shepherd of the Church in many lifetimes past, but I was also the main recorder who assembled the original Bible text and more given by the old prophets and placing them in hiding to keep them from the dark forces of the church until such time that we humans are ready to receive the truth. And here I am today, working again with Jesus and the Ascended Masters to expose religion and the misguided rituals that keep their followers asleep to the real truth of you being the God and the Savior you seek.

According to Jesus, the written words in the Bible are only interpreted and understood as having several layered meanings, and it is up to each individual to awaken to the truth by way of incarnations, thereby reaching a vibrational signature (DNA-Divine Natural Attribute) where you become one with your own Christ consciousness as Jesus himself did. As one grows in wisdom because of reincarnation, one will eventually learn the wisdom behind the text, as it refers to you as Christ, God, and the Goddess.

Therefore, the prophets of old and those that recorded the words through time and space wrote these literal words to have multiple frequency meanings to hide the true wisdom behind them because of religion's dark forces desiring to maintain their power and control over the people. And now, the day has come where these words and text can be revealed and understood from a consciousness frequency that is awakened to the deception and lies of the church.

The Bible was written in this way because it was the only way to hide the real truth about Christ from these dark-minded leaders of the church until such a time that we would rise and see what has been happening to us. And, when the time is right, we will awaken to this multi-dimensional formula of ascending to the real truth about "Christ" and that "God" is not a person or a deity, but is as a "universal omnipresent mind field of pure unbiased energy of light" that we humans use for our creations.

Like many of you, I have gone through many lifetimes experiencing great deals of pain and suffering. And after many incarnations playing as a Shepherd to the Church, I finally reached a lifetime as a Sheikh who spoke loudly against the Church teachings, and in doing so, I was burned at the stake by the church. This explains why I was shy and feared this God of the Bible, priests, and those having authority in my early years growing up.

It also explains why, in early 1975, the Monks had the Angelic Realm's blessings to come and inform me that it was meant for me to awaken to the real truth in this lifetime. It was the prelude of Jesus' special message to me in 2013. However, this time around, I will not be put to death by some church because I have the "Keys of the Kingdom," where I am fully aware of their false teachings, and at the same time, protected by the divine spirit of Christ.

Working with religion in so many previous lifetimes as one of them, and learning about their misguided teachings, gave me the wisdom that eventually awakened me to the real Christ, the Christ within me.

Even now, Jesus, Lord Melchezidek, the Archangels, and the Ascended Masters do not judge or keep me to any vows or commitments that I may have made in some past lifetime working with religion because now I am an Ascended Master in my own right working out of a fifth-dimensional consciousness and not out of a three-dimensional consciousness here on earth.

What I write as blogs, books, and my experiences here on earth are not about any commitment to Jesus or any religion but a commitment to myself as a Christ in my own right. All choices that I make come from the sovereignty of my Christ consciousness and not from my mind that is emotional and blinded by this world's dark forces, such as the media, large businesses, the religions of the world, and our politicians.

I have learned that each lifetime stands on its own, and all that we do as a Christ, Gods, and as Goddesses is to suck the nectar of wisdom that comes from each lifetime's choice and experience. And, this is why in this lifetime, as a disciple of my own Christ consciousness, I can bring forth the wisdom of all those lifetimes and more to those that dare to hear it.

From Socrates's words of wisdom: *"The truly free individual is free only to the extent of his own self-mastery. While those who will not govern themselves are condemned to find masters to govern them."*

Chapter 6

THE FOUR BUILDING BLOCKS OF GOD

It was October 2013, and after my wife and I had retired for the night, we both suddenly heard loud noises coming from the foyer area of the front door. So much so, my wife asked if I wouldn't mind getting up from bed to check the door to see if it was locked. Feeling a little anxious myself, I got up from the bed and walked into the foyer area. And as I approached the front door to check the lock, I began to feel some commanding but gentle energies around me.

Knowing the lock was secure, I then understood the noise we were hearing, and while returning to the bedroom, this commanding but gentle energy presence around me began to feel stronger and stronger. That is when I knew what we heard was a group of ascended masters coming for a visit. Then my wife and I began to hear the ascended masters move from the foyer area to climbing the staircase to my office. And with each step they took, the noise increased significantly. So, I yelled out to them to quiet down. Of course, my remark was humorous, for we both were giggling.

As the spirits reached the second floor, we heard them proceed down the hallway to my office, which is just above the master bedroom on the main level. Once they entered my office, they began to quiet down. That is when my wife and I realized that there must have been eight or nine spirits altogether. Of course, I surmised that the reason why they entered my office was to discuss the creation of another book.

It was right after they settled down that I began to notice three of them drifting down from the floor of my office above and directly into our bedroom below. As I was lying on the bed, I looked up and saw them floating down from the ceiling to our bedroom floor. That is when I noticed it was Jesus, Lord Melchizedek, and Archangel Michael. Once they had my attention, Lord Melchizedek began to speak to me about writing a special kind of book that reflects on the subject of Christ's return.

After the message was given to me, Lord Melchezidek then gave me the names of the spirits that were upstairs in my office, waiting to help me write the new book. My office is where I write my books, so that is why they went upstairs instead of coming directly into the bedroom. They just allowed the group leaders to handle the message. Before I go on, I should mention that before writing this unique book, the ascended masters had already logged in and had helped me write three other books since 2013. These books were founded on the "Book of Genesis," the "Book of Revelation," and the "Fall of the Church."

And, here I am now, about seven years later, with Lord Melchezidek, Jesus, and the group has stopped by again to help me write this special book on the subject of God, Christ's return, the Rapture, the lies, and how this book will be for those that are ready to ascend to the fifth-dimensional consciousness. From what you have read so far, you can see how special this book can be for those with the eyes to see, the ears to hear, and the wisdom to be mindful of what these angelic beings desire to convey to you about Christ and of you moving into a fifth-dimensional consciousness.

So, here we are in this section of the book, Chapter 6, and Jesus and the Ascended Masters are going to present to you the "Four Building Blocks of God." However, know that it is essential to distinguish between these "Four Building Blocks of God" before you can ever understand Christ and Ascension. As known, the church has always made God, and the expression of the word itself, very confusing and mysterious because they want to maintain the illusion of this God of the Bible as coming from light when, in truth, this God comes from the dark.

This then allows the church to keep us asleep to the real meaning behind Christ's return and an understanding of the word "God." And by keeping us locked into a three-dimensional consciousness, where duality, along with this "God" being the rule of order, it prevents us from ever moving into the fifth dimension. And it is the fifth-dimensional consciousness where the true God and Christ are revealed.

To clear up any confusion about God, and to help us understand God better, Jesus and the ascended masters are going to voice their wisdom on what we understand as the "beginning." This will then help us understand the real God and the real Christ, as they relate to us souled beings on a higher divine level. Therefore, let it be known that the "beginning" was not about a Garden, or even Adam, Eve, the Serpent, or that of humankind entering Earth. It was about the consciousness of the Spirit of One.

Hence, the "beginning" is not about a white, male God that created the universe, humankind, and the earth as we appreciate these things to be. Instead, it was the "beginning of us souled beings becoming aware of our consciousness" as an acting force in all our creations. However, the word "beginning" and the word "God" themselves are not the appropriate words to use because, in truth, there was never a "beginning," nor was there a "God." It was an "awakening."

For instance, in terms of understanding all of this, one has to look at the Spirit of One's consciousness and how it was expressed and presented as being the Goddess, and the "oneness of all that was," was just us souled beings. In other words, we spirits were "all that was in consciousness" in the beginning and not some God as we understand God today; as we souled beings not only represent the Spirit of One in her absoluteness, infiniteness, limitlessness, and everlastingness, with having no beginning or end, we are also her consciousness, and she is our consciousness. Thus, the "beginning" and this "God," as we understand God to be, in their truest sense of the word, never was, because, according to Jesus and the Ascended Masters, what we call the "beginning" and "God" was, in fact, an act in "consciousness" where we souls began to recognize ourselves as the source.

Therefore, the "beginning" was not about something appearing out of nowhere, like the Universe or Adam, Eve, and the Garden, but was the activation of the Spirit of One's "awakening" to her own Consciousness where she recognized herself as being God, the Goddess, Christ, and "all that is, and ever will be," for her awakening to consciousness became known as the "first creation" mentioned in the Bible. Of course, the term "first creation" is symbolic of the Garden and not that there was a real Garden in some heaven.

It is really about one's own divine Christ consciousness as representing "Heaven" and the "Goddess" within. The Garden, taken literally, was to help us understand "not only our beginning," but as in an awakening to our own Christ consciousness. Also, with our Christ consciousness, we, as souled beings, created the "beginning of neutralized Energy," which is also expressed and known to us as "God." Thus, there was no God, and if there is no God, then there is no Devil, no earth, no universe, no ego-personality aspect, and no energy with this "first awakening."

However, within a blink of an eye, or instantaneously, we souled beings (all gazillions upon gazillions of us), acting as the Spirit of One, followed in that awakening, like a microsecond afterward, created what the church calls God and Jesus and the Ascended Masters call "universal neutralized energy of no force." And in that awakening, we souls, at first, had no division, no positive, no negative, no gender, and no name or form to us.

We souled beings, acting as the Spirit of One, didn't even have weight, height, size, or that we were part of time and space; for there was only our Consciousness for which the Garden symbolizes. In fact, nothing existed outside of our Christ Consciousness because all that existed was just consciousness. There were no stars, universes, planets, animals, vegetation, moons, or anything of an energy nature that the Spirit of One (us souled beings) could interact with other than our Christ Consciousness.

But, once the Spirit of One, or us souled beings, acting together as one, became aware of our Christ Consciousness, we instantaneously asked ourselves a question: "Who am I?" And it was from this single question, we souls ended up generating a mirror image of ourselves in order to see ourselves. And, with this "act in consciousness," the desire to express caused us to bring forth what is called today "God and light." Therefore, the "Garden" the church speaks of is symbolic of our "Christ Consciousness."

In other words, the Spirit of One and "all that was in the beginning," if we want to call it that, was us souled beings triggering our own awakening in consciousness as the source of life and the creator of all that is, and not that some God created us. In fact, it was with this "act in consciousness" by us souled beings, in that moment of great passion in answering the question, "Who Am I?", we fragmented our "oneness of consciousness" into many, many parts and pieces of ourselves. And in doing so, we set the pattern in creating a divine plan to learn who we are as divine beings. (Genesis 3:5)

This means that every souled being, meaning you and me, and every human, are equal to whom religions call God. Allow me, as a disciple of Christ, to explain what is said here. First, the Garden is symbolic of us souled beings being the makeup of the "consciousness of the Spirit of One," also known as the Christ consciousness. Therefore, we are absolutely divine, and we had no beginning other than having an awakening that felt it was a "beginning."

And once we became awakened to our consciousness and existence, we instantly were given everything that the Spirit of One had: individuality, infiniteness, absoluteness, unlimited abilities, divineness, and the total freedom to express, love, experience, and choose our own fate as a real live and sovereign Goddess. Therefore, as understood by the church as to whom God is, we souled beings resided as a Goddess, individualized, but as one consciousness acting as the "Spirit of One" in creating a divine plan to learn "who we are" as an "omnipresent consciousness" (meaning we actually have a consciousness that is present everywhere at once).

And this is what makes us souls a divine being and a Christ also, for we are everlasting and absolute equal in nature as far as having the authority to do whatever we please as a true living Goddess in our own right. And since we souled beings had all the Spirit of One's attributes, we had the authority to give ourselves the "free will" to choose and the authority to create energy to feel our creations.

Thus, we souled beings then created what is known by Jesus and the Ascended Masters, is an "Omnipresent Universal Mind Field of Pure Absolute Neutralized Unbiased Energy" that ended up appearing as "light." And that is when this neutralized transparent energy became known as the "God of Light."

In other words, if there is "dark," then it had to come from "light," which means "dark" is an illusion. In short, Jesus and the ascended masters call this "God of Light" "Crystalline Energy," as it represents the "Father God" marrying up with the Goddess (or our "I AM" Christ consciousness). And together, we, as an individual Christ being, and as a group, created "all that is and ever will be." And, once I heard this clarification coming from Jesus and the Ascended Masters, that is when I understood the meaning behind what Jesus said to me in a channel concerning God. As his words were:

"God is like a vast ocean, and us humans are the drops of water making up that ocean; and, if we took away all the drops, then there would be no ocean, therefore no God." Hearing this statement from Jesus, and what has been said above about God being as an "energy of light," and not as a super male deity, we can now understand that it took the Goddess part of our Christ consciousness to create this "God of Light," which is just transparent energy, but an energy that is neutralized, and with complete unbiasedness, is absolutely unchangeable, and infinite. Therefore, it was us souled beings who created God and not the other way around.

It also shows that God is not a single-minded white male deity that is the creator of "all that is," but is an "omnipresent mind field of pure absolute, unbiased neutralized energy," called "Crystalline Energy," which happens to appear as "light." Haven't you heard the expression that "God is Light?" Therefore, according to Jesus and the Ascended Masters, we are, in our natural form, a Christ, a Goddess, and we use God (this "Neutralized Energy of Light") for our creations. This is where the misinterpretation of sin comes from since we souls used this pure energy of neutrality (God) to create an energy that spirals in a manner that feels opposite to pure and neutral.

Hence, nothing can happen in physical life, right, wrong, good or evil, light or dark, poorness, richness, health, or unhealthiness unless it happens first within our own consciousness. And yet, our consciousness is, was, and has always been infinite, having no beginning or end, and that consciousness part of us is the Goddess and the creator of what we experience in life.

Therefore, what we understand as the Devil is nothing more than one's building up of one's ego-personality, not believing one is a Goddess, the Christ, and the creator of our world. It came from our awakening in spirit consciousness eons ago that we automatically set in motion a divine plan to "know all that there is to know" about this Neutralized Energy that appeared as Light that we souled beings created to use for our creations and our experiences.

And in that creation of Energy that we happen to call God, we began the set up for us souls to split this "Crystalline Energy of Light" into an Energy of Two (light and dark). In other words, we souls, acting as the Spirit of One, eons ago, and by way of a "consciousness act," split this "Crystalline Energy" and generated (created) what the masters call "Crystal Energy." And from this creation, we souls produced a new form of "energy" that seemed to appear as "light and dark," where one part of it spiraled upward in the opposite direction from the other side.

And from this, "Crystal Energy of Light and Dark," and with its formula as appearing as opposites, we ended up creating a new type of energy called "Cosmic Energy." And it was from this "Cosmic energy of light and dark," we all ended up formulating a mental version of what appeared as "light and dark" energy to appear as to oppose each other where we now come to earth as a male or female. That was when we souls then set up a formulated emotional creation called the "Mind" and our "Soul Record of Responsibility," which is symbolized by Adam and Eve in the Garden.

Adam represented the masculine-positive-light side of the mind, and Eve took on the opposite role, represented by the feminine-negative-dark side of that same mind. And together, it all represents the "tree of knowledge of good and evil." And yet, this Cosmic Energy of Light and Dark just represents our mental mind (Adam) and our soul (Eve) partaking of dual thinking and manifesting what comes to us in opposites, like positive and negative. Thus, none of what we call good and evil, right and wrong, light and dark, and positive and negative are actually real. All symbolized by the apple!

It was from this "act in consciousness" by the gazillions upon gazillions of us souled beings working on an emotional level mimicking what we did in creating "Crystalline Energy (expressed as God)" where we ended up creating an outer version of ourselves that came in the form of a dual-energy and dual-consciousness. And it was from this "dual mental consciousness" where we souls ended up creating what is called "Earth Energy." And with this "Earth Energy," we souls produced an energy of such density and polarity, our consciousness took on another layer of itself that ended up as our ego-personality consciousness that became physical and lost (asleep) to our higher Christ Consciousness.

And from this lower vibrating three-dimensional consciousness, along with a three-dimensional energy of duality, we souls ended up as being the fallen angels described in the Bible as Satan's army in opposing our own Christ consciousness. And, this is where the church gets its idea of everyone being born with sin. Of course, this is a false idea, as Jesus and the Ascended Masters declare that there is no such thing as sin, only experiencing to gain wisdom from our choices playing with the illusion of light and dark in order to learn the wisdom behind one being Christ. And, in the end, we eventually find our way back to the oneness of consciousness again.

When an idea (thought) is born from within our mind, our mental consciousness desires to materialize it using dense energy to experience the idea through our five physical senses. However, before the mind can service this idea and materialize it, such as having a physical body, the energy first must come from Crystalline Energy of neutrality. And once the idea moves through our mental-emotional mind, a choice has to be made on what energy frequency we want the idea to be played out, either mentally using cosmic energy or physically using earth energy. Therefore, once we souls enter earth as a newborn, that is when the mind of man chooses to use either positive, negative, or neutral energy as the basic configuration to play out the idea to experience.

In other words, do we choose to play it out as good, bad, or play it out in a neutralized, compassionate, unconditional state of mind in the flesh? Remember, we souls created not only Crystalline Energy, which is divine neutralized energy, we also created Crystal, Cosmic, and Earth Energy that vibrates in a dualistic way and in a different frequency. And once we souls began to lean more toward desiring to experience both sides of a coin in a more outrageous observation, or the opposite of neutral or unconditional, and because of how our emotional mind works, we began to choose more of Cosmic and Earth Energy as our basic source for our creations. Thus, we became more conditional than unconditional with our creations.

In other words, from mankind's perspective, we have a hard time distinguishing the whole idea of there only being Crystalline Energy because of forgetfulness. Therefore, we only see Earth Energy as being all that there is. We souled beings have forgotten that Crystal, Cosmic, and Earth Energy all come from Crystalline Energy. But because of our mental and emotional nature, we only understand energy as dualness, positive and negative, or good and evil. Therefore, Adam represents our masculine side of our mind, and Eve represents our feminine side. And the "tree of good and bad" in the Bible symbolizes Earth's dual-energy of positive and negative.

Adam took up the positive side because that is the side of our mind that makes choices, and Eve took up the mind's negative side, as she represents our soul consciousness of responsibility. What happens is, by way of our mental, emotional consciousness of responsibility (Eve), we record all of what we think and believe that comes into our masculine side of the mind (Adam) to choose what energy to use; positive, negative, or neutrality (unconditional) in manifesting those beliefs in order to experience them.

However, we are likely to use "Earth Energy" as our foundation because of our fall in consciousness to a three-dimensional consciousness. Of course, this eliminates the church's teachings of Eve, taking the first bite of the apple since that part of our mind records all thoughts to one's memory. And from there, our masculine side chooses as to one's creations being conditional or unconditional.

It will always be the masculine side of the mind (symbolized by Adam) that will first come up with the ideas, thoughts, and beliefs about what one desires to experience in life. And Eve will always be there in memory to remind us of our responsibility when it comes to our thoughts, choices, and energy manifestations. Thus, Adam was the first to take the bite of the apple and not Eve. Eve only recorded what Adam was thinking and then passed the thought back to Adam to choose.

However, since most here on earth are part of a three-dimensional consciousness, it does not matter if one chooses positive or negative. Why? Because the energy used has already been tainted because of the mind of man accepting the belief in a God that is good and a Devil that is evil. And as long as we belong to a three-dimensional consciousness, one will always experience light and dark creations as if real because of the authority (power) placed behind the creation.

Remember, you are God, Christ, and a Goddess, and if you, at your core essence, feed your ego-consciousness with the belief in good and evil, then, because of your authority as a Christ, you will manifest that experience to play out no matter if good or evil. Why is this? It is because of man's deep belief in separation, sin, and punishment.

This strong belief in sin is what kicked us, souls, out of our higher divine Christ consciousness of neutrality in the first place. And this is why we, as humankind, live out of an ego-personality consciousness that believes in power, which is why we participate in a wavering, interacting, dualistic "Earth Energy" frequency that is so dense and opposing, we feel and experience it as something real, and yet it is not real.

From what we created in the beginning as this "universal omnipresent mind field of pure neutralized energy of light," we souls ended up manipulating this "God Energy of Light" into what is called by the masters the "Four Building Blocks of God." Thus, initiating not only "time and space," but an avenue for us souls to experience all kinds of potentials and dimensions filled with good and evil, and some dimensions filled with nothing but unconditional love as an individual Goddess to learn wisdom. In other words, to learn how to be a God, Christ, and a Goddess.

It was we souled beings, acting and working together as the Godhead that created "all that we see and experience today," even what we all call evil in this world. And this includes creating many dimensions, universes, stars, planets, moons, plants, animals, physical bodies, the fish of the seas, and much, much more, for everything that lives and or dies come from us souled beings using dual-energy in materializing it to experience. Therefore, God's name as God became the very system in which our soul was lost in a world of dense and opposing energy that is not even real, which is why this God of the Bible is not real.

However, we keep it real because we call it sin. It was not sin! It was just us souled beings moving in many different directions and dimensions all at the same time; from neutrality to positive, then to negative, and back to neutrality, all leading us souls to be trapped in a playing field of energy where both light and dark, good and evil, positive and negative, felt real to us without realizing it as an illusion. Crystalline Divine Energy is the only energy that is not an illusion. Thus, the real God and the real Goddess is our consciousness!

By moving our consciousness in many different energy directions and dimensions, it moved us into believing that duality is "all that is," which is why we believe this God of the Bible is real. And in the end, we lost our true heritage by neglecting our neutrality state of being as "all that is." This opened the door for those that love power to come in and control us by mind programming. And we allowed it by launching a powerful, dense "Earth Energy" and labeled everything as light and dark, good and evil, right and wrong, God and Satan, and sin and punishment. Thus, all becoming our primary belief system. And now, we are asleep to what we did!

Therefore, the God that religion has taught us about for centuries, according to Jesus and the Ascended Masters, is a false god, and therefore not our creator or deity that we need to worship. As we are all disciples of Christ, only those of a three-dimensional consciousness will follow this false God.

What needs attention is our "I AM" Christ Consciousness, along with other "I AM" Goddesses, as we together, were the ones that created this "universal omnipresent mind field of pure neutralized unbiased energy of light" that later took the composition as appearing as "four differing energies." And yet, these energies are still one, just as we are one!

These "Four Building Blocks of God" are:

i. Crystalline Energy (pure, neutral, infinite, having no dualness or opposite to it, and is the core energy that our "I AM" Christ Goddess consciousness uses in the creation of all energies)

ii. Crystal Energy (pure, neutral, having a slight dualness to it, and we hardly use it because of it not having the same purity as our core neutral energy)

iii. Cosmic Energy (mental, emotional, and made up of opposing energy, and is the building block of the universe, such as time and space)
iv. Earth Energy (very dense and very much opposing, and is the ninety-eight percent of what we humans use for our creations on earth).

It took us, souls, in human form over billions and billions of years to fall into this sleep state of not knowing we are Goddesses and Christ beings in disguise using energy (God) in manifesting our creations. And it has been taking billions of years, via through reincarnation, to awaken to the wisdom of it all. And yet, there are billions of us still physically earthbound playing in a three-dimensional consciousness sound asleep. And we also have those souls belonging to the non-physical dimensional realms that are now ready to reach their final lifetime to awaken to "who they are."

Chapter 7

THE GARDEN OF EDEN

Religion has taught for centuries that the Garden of Eden is a place where God created Adam and Eve to live a life of utopia, but only if they remain faithful and true to God and his declaration not to eat the fruit of the "tree of knowledge of good and evil." But as the Bible proclaims, Adam and Eve chose to eat the forbidden fruit, which supposedly triggered their expulsion from the Garden. However, was this expulsion over defiance, or was it to experience the opposite of what they were experiencing as utopia?

First of all, since the masters have already established that Adam, Eve, and the Serpent are symbolic in representing our mind, our soul, our ego, and the "Four Building Blocks of God (Energy of Light), then know they and all souled beings were already part of the Garden, before the eating of the forbidden fruit as prescribed by the Bible. Therefore, how can it be a sin or defiance if, from our "I AM" Christ consciousness, symbolic of the tree of life, we souls chose a material existence to create experiences that would allow us to play opposite roles than our natural state of neutrality and divineness to learn wisdom?

Remember, Adam symbolizes our masculine mental side of the mind; Eve, our soul, mental consciousness of responsibility; and the

Serpent as our defiant Cain ego-personality consciousness experiencing our choices. It wasn't until our "individualized ego" in challenging the deceptive side of our emotional and rational mind that we souls ended up exploring the "four building blocks of God." And this is where we began to experience duality and denseness. And simultaneously, to learn how far we could journey outside of our neutralized Christ consciousness. And it was all done to find the wisdom behind our choice in the creating of dense dual-energy.

In Geneses 3:10, when our mind of a masculine nature (Adam) answered God, *"I heard you in the Garden, but I was afraid because I was naked, so I hid myself."* This has nothing to do with being naked! It is about being exposed to "fear" for the very first time once we souled beings moved our focus from out of our own Christ Consciousness (Garden) to a much lower mental and soul consciousness that dealt with dual-energy as its source.

It is like this God of the Bible we all follow and believe who created us as our source, when in fact, this God is symbolic of a dual-energy where the frequency wave is so low, we souls ended up settling in a dense three-dimensional consciousness that caused us to forget who we are because of being exposed (naked) to an unknown dual-energy we all call God. However, since we are a Christ in our own right, then no matter how much we layered our consciousness of one, consciousness still comes from consciousness and not from a single God outside of ourselves.

Thus, this act of focusing our three-dimensional consciousness on fear and dual-energy that was unknown to us at the time exposed us to creating a deceitful and cunning Cain ego-personality of fear that eventually led us into a very dense physical consciousness of obscurity (forgetfulness) here on earth. The confirmation of this comes from Genesis 3:11, where the masculine side of our mind replied to God by saying, *"the woman whom you put here with me gave me the forbidden fruit to eat."*

This confirms how our feminine soul mental consciousness of record and responsibility was just feeding back to the Adam side of our mind what we already chose to manifest before literally eating the forbidden fruit, which is just symbolic of us feeding our mind with opposing energy instead of the neutralized pure divine energy deep within. This also proves that we souls were not ready emotionally to take responsibility for our expressions and thoughts, let alone our actions in our beginning stages of learning about consciousness and energy and this fear we were feeling inside.

The fear came from the unknownness that we may not return to our Christ consciousness, or at least until we explored all facets of our dualistic mind and soul, using the "Four Building Blocks of Energy (God of Light) to create our experiences. And when the masculine side of the mind (Adam) became one with our soul record of responsibility (Eve), symbolized by man and wife coming together as one, it generated a subconsciousness and an outer mental consciousness that ended up creating an ego-personality of defiance and a consciousness of awareness that Cain and Abel represent.

Therefore, through this defiant ego Cain personality of ours, we took on the belief in "dual-energy" (God of duality (good and evil)) that finally led us into the failure of taking full responsibility for our creations. We denied this responsibility because we did not understand that we already created and accepted, as part of us, an inner subconsciousness (feminine) to hold in memory all that we believe, think, and desire, and then using our outer masculine consciousness as the choosing consciousness for our manifested creations. But instead, we, the Adam side of our mind, decided to blame that part of our consciousness that was already part of our inner feminine soul record of responsibility (Eve), which then led to the blaming of our ego-serpent Cain personality consciousness. Thus, in the process, we failed to recognize that we were still "one consciousness."

What happened is that our defiant ego-personality consciousness felt individualized and separate from our Christ consciousness, our mind, and our soul consciousness of responsibility, and then had seen itself as having three different and opposing consciousnesses, so why not blame it on one of them. And this is why today we are called a three-dimensional being living in a three-dimensional world, believing that our Christ, Mind-Soul, and Ego consciousnesses are separate from us.

For example, do you believe you are Christ in the flesh? Remember, when the woman answered God in Genesis 3:13, *"saying the serpent tricked me into it, so I ate it?"* This is where we souls chose to descend into a lower consciousness frequency and then take on a belief that dual-energy (this God of opposing energy) was "all that was;" and that is when we souls ended up partaking in an energy of such a frequency, we ended up creating a very dense energy where we could experience opposite roles in a material form than just being transparent, neutral, and absolute.

This allowed us the opportunity to experience being male, female, black, brown, red, white, yellow, and many religions. Therefore, the question of dual-energy, individuality, our higher consciousness, and the experiencing of our defiant ego-personality was actually unknown to us in the beginning stages of creating opposite roles to experience. Hence, fear became a phobia so intense that it became part of every lifetime experience. And it still goes on today!

And this is why Jesus and the Ascended Masters are asking us to put all fear aside about being kicked out of the Garden because of sin. The Garden is nothing more than our consciousness is vibrating to many different frequencies and dimensions (in my father's house, there are many mansions) John14:2. Thus, in contrast, our defiant ego Cain personality consciousness operates at the lowest frequency, causing us to be unaware (asleep) of our many-layered consciousnesses that are spread throughout multiple dimensions.

In other words, we souls left our Christ consciousness on a voluntary challenge that actually came from our own Christ spirit and not that we were kicked out of any Garden. That is a myth and a misinterpretation by those who love to live by the Cain consciousness of jealousy, judgment, power, hatred, lies, murder, pedophilia, and the desire to control others at all costs.

However, before the Cain consciousness took control of the world, we souls, at first, felt on an emotional level to take the challenge, and we were excited about what this dual-energy could do for us as far as soul growth and wisdom. So, there we were, in our divine state, and before the fall into the Cain consciousness, we chose to leave our Christ consciousness to explore, develop, and expand our consciousness by playing with dual-energy (this God of opposites) and an ego-personality to learn the wisdom behind our choices.

We are even responsible for creating our own physical bodies and stories (lifetimes) to be played out as real, and yet, they are just an illusion, like a hologram, that feel real to learn the wisdom behind our acts. To really understand the challenge that was placed before us by our Christ consciousness, it was for us to learn the real truth about "who we truly are" as a sovereign God-Goddess in our own right. However, to meet that challenge, we souls needed something that would help us forget that we are a sovereign Goddess in our own right, having the same composition as the Spirit of One. Thus, our own Christ spirit helped us forget by introducing us to a cunning personality of a deceptive and egotistical nature where we would find ourselves focus in and around a mental mind believing it is separate from our Christ consciousness.

Of course, this focus on such a lower part of our consciousness, and without warning, we ended up producing a deep sensation that appeared as power. It was from this false perception that our ego-personality having power that caused us souls to generate a personality within us of control, jealousy, judgment, blame, and cleverness. And with these traits, we built up a shrewdness about us that was taken as ingenuity and intelligence on our part, which was actually artificial, but we believed it to be real. And all of this is symbolized by the Cain Principle.

From the deceptiveness coming from our mind-soul and ego, it placed us into a consciousness of forgetting, where we all ended up getting lost in an ego-personality aspect of ourselves where our education, knowledge, self-worth, and intelligence came from being taught to us instead of seeking the wisdom behind what we have already learned and experienced in other lifetimes. This lack of seeking on our part led to a doctrine that some God created us and that we were kicked out of a Garden.

That was when a new day was created, as the deceptive mental and emotional part of our consciousness caused friction between our Christ consciousness, our Abel awareness of knowing who we are at our core level, and the ego-personality within ourselves that decided to live by the Cain Principle. Thus, confirming the feeling of being separate from our Christ spirit seem real. This then caused us from a mental and ego level to feel that we souls were indeed separate and alone in the world, having no concept that together we still are the Spirit of One (God-Goddess) that created "all that there is," for nothing was or is left out, not even the creation of what we call God.

The "throne" that we are taught as being the "throne of God" is symbolic of every one of us souled beings (you, me, and everyone) having the same composition, power, rank, and privileges as the Spirit of One, because together, we are the Spirit of One. And therefore, equal to whom we call God-Goddess and not less than. Like Jesus, this is also why we were already in heaven (higher consciousness) before time, space, and physicality began.

As the Bible portrays Eve as taking a bite of the apple and then passing it on to Adam, it simply means that Eve, our soul record of responsibility, became the holder, like women carry a baby seeded by her husband, in what the outer deceptive mind (Adam) desires to experience, and with the help of our defiant Cain ego-personality as the tool in playing opposite roles in the flesh to learn the wisdom of our choices.

Remember, Adam and Eve became symbolic of our masculine and feminine mental part of our consciousness, and therefore they are transparent and not real people. In other words, we are all Adams and Eves playing out of our Cain and Abel ego-personality consciousnesses, as they are the consciousnesses that play in the physical realm where the Cain personality carries a low energy frequency that matches the earth's dense three-dimensional frequency while our Abel awareness consciousness carries a much higher frequency, even though we are in the flesh.

Therefore, to confirm that Adam was the first to bite the symbolic apple and not Eve is where she represents the soul in recording what Adam was thinking, and then passing that thought back to Adam to choose what consciousness and energy to use, either our Cain ego-personality or our Abel awareness ego-personality to play out in the flesh. This can be found in Genesis 3:14, *"Because you have done this, you are cursed more than all cattle, and more than every beast of the field; On your belly, you shall go, and you shall eat dust All the days of your life."*

As you can see in this verse, most of us have been choosing to work out of our defiant Cain ego-personality consciousness as the means to incarnate into the flesh playing out all kinds of fake good and evil deeds. Yet, after many incarnations, some of us are about to choose to work out of our Abel awareness consciousness that will propel us into the fifth dimension and more. Know that once one opens to the fifth dimension, one also has the opportunity to open to multiple dimensions.

It is to know that all thoughts, ideas, and desires come from our mind's deceptive side, the Adam side that gave life to a Cain ego-personality that works with the dark. In other words, it takes the outer rational mind (Adam) to begin the thought process and not our soul record of responsibility (Eve). Our soul record of responsibility (Eve) only records in memory the thoughts, ideas, and desires that come from the deceptive side of the mind (Adam). And it takes the Cain ego consciousness to play them out in the flesh. This is where religion teaches their narrative of how Adam was misled by Eve, which of course, is false. This is also why mankind (male and female) looks upon God as being a male persona even though technically, the God of the Bible is only a mental version of the real God, and therefore not real.

It is through religions and mankind looking upon this mental version of God as our creator. And yet, this God of the Bible is a false God because it is based on jealousy, revenge, good and evil, right and wrong, light and dark, sin and punishment, duality. God's real composition is only of a "universal omnipresent mind field of pure absolute, unbiased energy of light" that we souls used in creating this false God to experience duality, life, and the wisdom found in our choices.

The belief in this God of the Bible has caused the male gender to feel superior over the female, which is false. It feels that way because mankind (male and female) only works from out of their emotional and rational mind. And the feminine side of that same mind only records what the masculine side thinks and desires to experience. Thus, my friends, there is no such thing as sin! Why? Because our Christ spirit (Goddess-Oversoul-feminine side) had passed all power (authority) over to our outer deceptive divided mind where the masculine side (Adam) judge's thoughts as either good or evil and then stores them in memory (feminine side (Eve)) until such a time those judged thoughts are passed back to the masculine side of self to choose what to experience in any given lifetime to understand life.

The bottom line is that it took our own Christ consciousness (Goddess) and this "universal omnipresent mind field of pure unbiased energy of light" (God) that made it possible for us to create a whole new world of playing opposite roles, using dual-energy; like being a male in one lifetime and a female in the next, then experiencing the ups and downs, the good and bad, and physicality and non-physicality. This is also why we all have emotional ties to many of our past lifetimes that deal with family, enemies, phobias, religion, and many of our beliefs in things that don't even make sense today.

As we understand it, the essence of life, along with this "universal omnipresent mind field of pure unbiased energy of light," that we use to give our creations form and animation, is, in fact, the collectiveness of what religions call God. I want to quote a passage from Adamus Saint-Germain's book, "Act of Consciousness," channeled and written by Geoffrey and Linda Hoppe of Crimson Circle. In fact, I would recommend buying this book at www.crimsoncircle.com.

"The soul is like the sun, up there just shinning away, rather oblivious to what's happening down here on earth. It really doesn't have an agenda other than to shine. It loves shining. It shines all day and all night. It shines all the time, whether you can see it or not, and doesn't care if the trees and the grass accept its light."

"It doesn't care whether you get sunburned or protect yourself from its rays. The sun doesn't care if it's too hot or if something is blocking its warmth. It's just there in its radiance and expression. Its passion is to shine. It doesn't differentiate between a good day or a bad day. It doesn't even know it's a day. It just is, always shining."

That's how our own Christ consciousness operates as it is there, always illuminating its presence without us realizing it.

Chapter 8

BELIEF SYSTEMS

Belief systems became the tool for us to create our experiences, good and bad. But, before we discuss belief systems, let's speak about how we souls, in our awakening eons ago, took on a mirror likeness of our Christ Consciousness in our awakening eons ago. In other words, we, at first, had no physical body or a deceptive mental body that we could see with our eyes or touch with our fingers because, in the first awakening, we were nothing but spirit, consciousness, expression, and light. It wasn't until we split our consciousness from an absolute pure and neutralized consciousness to a dual mental consciousness where we initiated our first belief, which was fear, all because of feeling our existence outside of who we truly are at our core.

Even though we had no form other than light in the first creation, we somehow knew that we could think and create images of things because of our mental consciousness. That is where we souls, for the very first time, felt that we wanted to experience something, anything, no matter if it was right or wrong because it made no difference to us. Of course, the question was, how can we experience something if we are only consciousness, expression, and light?

That was when we, for the first time, began to express more and more of our thoughts outward and into what was nothingness (the

Bible calls the abyss). Jesus and the ascended masters called it the "second creation." However, even today, we have forgotten that our Christ spirit has never ventured beyond the "first creation." Thus, it is only a mental perception on our part.

By moving into this "second creation," as it was called our mental imaging realm, where we could image things but only in a translucent way. That was when we asked, "What is the purpose of our mental-soul region of consciousness? And, the answer was, "How could we ever come to learn wisdom and feel our creations if we can only imagine what we desire to experience from a mental level?" And, as you can see, the answer was found that we could not, which is why we souls chose to move beyond the gates of our divine consciousness, known as the "first creation," or what is called our Christ consciousness to find the answer.

Therefore, we left the "first creation" (higher consciousness) on purpose and chose to understand our thoughts about imaging things from a mental level to experience by creating a level of consciousness that would play in solid form. We did not just want to imagine things to experience. We wanted to manifest things to feel the experience to learn the wisdom behind it! So, by creating belief systems and dual-energy with such denseness, we gave ourselves the ability to learn, feel, touch our creations, and then acquire the byproduct of learning the wisdom behind these experiences. Thus, it became appropriate for us to create a divine plan (path or journey) where we souls would leave our Christ Sovereignty and move into a mental consciousness to understand materialism.

Therefore, it had nothing to do with Adam and Eve disobeying God. It was for out of love for our own Christ consciousness that we souls, in our deceptive mental and physical state of mind, would then share those experiences with our Christ spirit and with our soul brothers and sisters as we experience them in the flesh. Again, sin is just symbolic of a person who is asleep from understanding God as an energy source we soul's use in our creations to experience life and learn wisdom.

After the birth of power, we souls claimed this power as real and a reliable force to be reckoned with. Later, as we souls moved upon the earth's surface in a perceptual mental and physical mind and body, we misunderstood this power to be inclusive in scope to only this single solitary white male God of the Bible. And, when we looked upon this God as "all-knowing" and "all-powerful," and to the point that this God, at will, can destroy, protect, heal, and defend us, that was the time we felt our divine plan come into action.

It was and is still happening today because we humans keep trying to understand the external forces of life and our environment as something of a powerhouse system; we see this God of the Bible as the creator of the universe, the stars, the sun, the planets, earth, and all the plants, animals, and trees. And yet, it was us souled beings, acting as the Godhead that gave them life.

Why is there air to breathe, water to drink, food to eat, and many other things we all enjoy and need for our physical existence? And since we did not understand its whys, we, as souls, adopted many belief systems as a group consciousness. And one of those beliefs turned out to be an illusionary single solitary white male God as the creator of it all. We even accredit our skills, talents, appearance, intelligence, and all that benefits us on earth as coming from the belief and the worshipping of a false male God that has nothing to do with our appearance, talents, skills, our food, the possessions we own, our kinship to friends and family, and what we accumulate as wealth.

For those reasons, we define our reality and shape our world based upon this strong belief in an illusionary white male Hebrew God that was actually created by those in power to keep us as servants to them. We pray to this false God for peace, help, protection, and for our miracles, and what do we get? We get more problems, more wars, less freedom and protection, and no miracles. Why? It is because of our strong belief in this false god.

We are very much unaware that those things come from within ourselves in what we imagine to experience, for we, each one of us, are the creator of it all. What has been forgotten since we souls left the "first creation" (our Christ consciousness) and moved into the "second creation" (our perceptual mental consciousness), along with many battles with our soul brothers and sisters over control and power, was that we created multiple dimensions of an etheric nature that have become so intertwined with each other that we souls ended up creating a solid universe consisting of earth and a sensory-perceptual mental image of a God-like being that created it all. And we did all this without even realizing that we did it through belief systems.

At first, these ethereal dimensions were filled with expressions of feelings and thought patterns until we finally found ourselves in a place of consciousness where we created the illusion of light and dark, also known as positive and negative. This light and dark experience amazed us to where we could make things happen very fast, like magic, all because of the strong belief in power and how we could imagine things as fast as lightning. And with our strong belief in power, we souls from this etheric level of consciousness became very overwhelmed with how we could separate light and dark into whatever perceptional result we wanted to experience.

It was amazing and very noticeable that as fast as we could express a thought pattern, light or dark, it would appear before us as fast as we thought it possible. With the persistence of creating belief systems due to linking everything to our perceptual and rational mind, and the action of carrying them out, and with every experience we could imagine, no matter if it was good and evil, we carried them out as if they were real. And once this was done, we then filled those etheric dimensions with every possible potential, question, and occurrence, along with every possible answer and outcome.

We even did the same for every choice, as we created every possible solution to those choices. In fact, for every possible illness, sadness, relationship, war, worry, financial problems, and more, for it is endless, there is a solution to everything because we souls created it and stored it away in all those dimensions, including within our own memory. We even created a divine plan back to our own Christ consciousness, which is why once we enter the fifth dimension, we can move to higher dimensions. We just forgot we could do this because we keep on tripping over our many fabricated beliefs that we have taken on as our truths and how they have created our reality today.

It was and still is the use of belief systems that enabled us to take on physical bodies a long time ago in order to experience life, and in return, learn the wisdom of our choices. By accepting the process of using belief systems as the means to transform etheric energy into very dense and solid energy, it gave us the avenue to move away from just imagining what our experiences would feel like to where we could hear, touch, taste, smell, and see those experiences first hand. But once we enabled our belief systems to transform us into a tangible form (physical body), we became very confused when we returned to a non-physical form after just living out a current lifetime.

Therefore, to understand the process of having a physical life on earth, we souls began to create many ego personality-aspects of the self where each lifetime carries within them their own belief systems, agendas, and matters to play out in the physical. This is why we humans on earth experience a lot of suffering because deep within, we are battling with many belief systems that do not make sense anymore, but we hang onto them because of ancestral karma.

Remember, even though we live a lifetime here on earth feeling like it is all that we are in this lifetime, we are playing out many lifetimes simultaneously but just in a different dimension. And it is time to become aware of that because of our strong belief in good and evil, duality, in this lifetime. The belief in it is actually coming from our many past lifetimes. That is what keeps us trapped in a consciousness that only portrays life as to "who we believe we are in physical form" and not "who we truly are," a spirit having a human experience.

This means there is no colored race, no religion, no male or female, and no one is better than another. For example, because we have strong beliefs in good and evil, right and wrong, democrat and republican, God and Satan, Sin and Punishment, male and female, and that we are a bonafide sinner at birth, it makes us feel less than a Christ. Thereby, we overlook our authority as a Christ, of which we give away to others through trickery by saying one is black, brown, red, white, and yellow, male and female.

Of course, what is difficult here and why it could take many lifetimes to clear ourselves from old beliefs is that our perceptional mind's initial reaction to this, because of brainwashing, is to jam us right back into our old way of thinking because it seems unnatural to believe otherwise, like for an example, democrat or republican. Again, this is why we seem to never get away from our wars, hate, and suffering. It is because we all have been brainwashed by those that love to keep us under their control.

We may believe on the outside that we make choices all the time. However, on the contrary, we are not making choices as you believe because ninety-five percent of our choices come from our memories of many past lifetimes where they (our past lifetime aspects) have been misled and tricked into believing in a God of duality that loves us conditionally, hates us if we do wrong, judges us because of sin, and then punishes us because of being independent. This is how religion and the dark forces control our actions even after death. So, the question that needs asking, "How do we stop this process where our past lifetime aspects stop serving themselves because of their misguided beliefs and start serving us in our current lifetime on a more spiritual level?"

First, we must understand that our Christ consciousness has no agenda or desire other than to experience itself through our current lifetime. Therefore, if we believe in sin, hell, the color of our skin is real, good, and evil, or that we are unworthy of being a Christ, then that is the seed that our perceptional mind will nourish in what we experience here on earth as our reality. Second! If we hope to have a great life because of our strong faith in a God that lives outside of us and who created us, protects us, and gives us things because of that faith, then hope and faith can last lifetimes just because we send the seed of hope and faith outside of us as being the method of manifestation instead of realization, trust in self, and choice being the method to make it happened within first.

In other words, as long as we believe in hope as being our vehicle for success and health, which is nothing other than a wish, our perceptional mind and soul consciousness of responsibility will produce a reality that will match that hope as being someday in the future where God will heal us of our suffering. Therefore, to stop this chain of suffering, it is best to put "hope" and "someday" behind us all because of how it originates outside of ourselves first.

If our many past lifetime aspects hold to these beliefs of duality being real, like the color of our skin or what country or religion we were born into, in that case, those past lifetime aspects will always choose our current reality under the disguise of hope, a false faith, and sin. Once we understand that every one of us is the creator God-Goddess and the Christ of our beliefs and reality; then, the only thing that will give us what we desire in our current lifetime is the decision to allow ourselves to open up our consciousness to understand that "we are not who we believe we are," for we are more. A Christ in the flesh!

Remember, again, we are not our skin color, our vocation, and we are not our religion. We are not even our past lifetimes, our mind, body, or even a male or female; we are only of spirit, consciousness, expression, light (pure energy), and a Christ also. It is about going from an outside hope and who we believe we are to the "realization" that we are Christ in the flesh.

We have become so hypnotized and brainwashed by the world's elites, such as governments, religions, media, big businesses, and our politicians, by believing that one race is better than another, or Democrats are better than Republicans, or blue eyes are better than brown eyes, or vice versa, and that Socialism and Communism are better than Capitalism. Thus, we are dead to all that is real. Just allowing others' beliefs to control what we should do personally, in truth, takes away our sovereignty as a Christ and as a spiritual being.

Without realizing it, we have become so occupied with our beliefs regarding our government on all levels, what is believed to be the truth about God, according to our religions, and what seems real is real. All of which keeps us trapped in a world of deception, trickery, and delusions that we take as our truths without even questioning any of them as genuine.

Because of our physical body density, we only see what the brain understands as something that appears solid, and therefore it must be real and genuine. Therefore, if the brain only understands things as solid and real, then the eyes have no choice to see what is understood by the brain as solid and real, even though science will tell you nothing is solid or real. If the brain is filled with hardwired beliefs with what we perceive as truth and nothing but the truth, how can we see beyond what we believe is real?

We all have been taught for centuries that we must have a purpose in life. Even the human mind has been conditioned to believe that it has to have a purpose; otherwise, nothing is real. Most of us have set goals for ourselves in order to get out of bed in the morning so we can serve our purpose on earth. If this is so, then one would believe that life has a meaning. What if Jesus and the Ascended Masters say that there is actually no purpose or meaning to life? What would be your thoughts on that statement?

Many may say that Jesus or any Ascended Master would never say that life has no meaning or purpose. I know that many would say that we must have a meaning and a purpose in life; otherwise, what is the point of being here on earth? And I would somewhat agree with them! However, I can also see the point of Jesus and the Ascended Masters in their analogy. In other words, from Adamus Saint Germain's book, the "Act of Consciousness," channeled and written by Geoffrey and Linda Hoppe of the Crimson Circle, Adamus states:

"When there is no purpose, then there's no reason to try to find the meaning of life. The more you try to find it, the less you will actually discover. Life was not intended to have meaning. It was intended to be a playground of experiences to learn wisdom." This confirms the statement, "we are spirits having a human experience," and not that we are a "human having a spiritual experience." Because of our rational mind being hardwired to our memories from past lifetimes, the rational mind became a complex tool where we used it for a variety of different tasks and functions. Judgment became a way to help us remember things, like not to jump off high places or put our hand in a fire because it could lead to death or hurting ourselves.

We can all agree that the rational mind became a good source for information, like remembering things to help us survive or hold dearly to our hearts what we feel is important. This, of course, was good until someone figured out that we can use the rational mind to inject power into our many ideas, beliefs, and positions on any given subject. Significantly, the elites injecting a God of duality and the institution they work for as an expert in rendering God's words as truth and nothing but the truth.

For Example: Religion's interpretation of God is to move us toward a belief that we are created in his image, a God that we must worship, and a God that has given us rules (laws) to submit to without examining those rules beyond what we call duality and humanism as something outside of our divine sovereignty as a Christ. As most can attest to this thinking, it opens the door for those in power, like governments, religions, businesses, the media, and yes, even our parents and friends, to come into our space and influence us on what they believe is best for us.

We all can witness this today as our religions, the media, big businesses, and our politicians keep eroding away our freedoms through what they call science and to keep us safe. A great example of this is those in power creating tools like credit cards and other means to keep us in debt and in fear to where people are willing to give up their freedoms in exchange for the government to step in and help, not realizing more and more the elites are eroding away our sovereignty as a human being.

The mask is another excellent example, as we, the people, have a God-given right to breathe fresh air. The people would be shocked to learn about how much freedom we, constitutionally and spiritually, have lost in the last twenty or thirty years by dictatorial politicians and religions who have affected our sovereignty as citizens to spirit just by telling us that it is for our safety.

Chapter 9

THE EGO SEIZED ALL POWER AND CONTROL

(under the guise of a Cain consciousness)

When we began our journey as an extension of the Spirit of One, her omnipresent universal consciousness (present everywhere at once) became our consciousness, thus bequeathing us souls as the Mother-Goddess, the Christ, and the creator of "all that is today," including what is known as a "universal omnipresent mind field of pure neutralized unbiased energy of light," that Jesus called Father, and we humans misuse as God. Henceforth, each one of us owns their "God Energy of Light." In other words, no one else owns your share of this "God Energy of Light" but you.

However, one can steal your God's energy by having you believe that some God above and outside of you created you, and that good and evil are real, and therefore you need saving and protection. No one is higher than you or knows what is best for you because you are God, Goddess, and a Christ unto yourself. And when we as a group consciousness act as one, we have created and will create "all that is and ever will be." And when we believe, follow, and worship a God of duality, judgment, sin, and punishment (essentially all churches, teachers, and ministers), our authority as a Christ is lost to others and to those of a Cain consciousness.

Feeling our independence as a souled being in the fragmenting of the Spirit of One eons ago, not only did we all create a mind and an energy of duality (false God), but in the process of that creation, we developed what is called an ego-personality to feel our independence from our mind and our Christ consciousness. Thus, through what is called time and space, incarnation after incarnation, we layered our consciousness into a three-dimensional consciousness to fulfill our divine plan to experience "all that there is to experience," both good and evil, to learn the wisdom of our choices. And yet, we still all remain as "one consciousness."

In other words, because of your focus on the mental level in the first creation, you perceived yourself as having a spirit (Christ consciousness), mind-soul consciousness (mental), and an ego-consciousness (personality) where those layered consciousnesses felt separated from each other. And through your ego-consciousness, you lost sight of being aware of the Christ consciousness within and the control over your mind-soul by giving away your free will and your higher awareness to your Cain consciousness.

You can now understand why the Bible states that the "serpent" in the Garden was the most cunning of all (Genesis 3:1), as this consciousness represents your deceiving Cain consciousness working against your Abel consciousness of being aware that you are a Christ also. Thus, you moved from a higher state of consciousness eons ago to a three-dimensional consciousness where you, through time and space, incarnation after incarnation, created many ego type Cain-personality aspects of yourself that worked in an opposing way where you ended up becoming a multi-dimensional being, having multiple opposing beliefs and lifetimes. And it was all due to this layering of your consciousness and the ego's cunningness of having a Cain type of personality where you ended up becoming the "beast" mentioned in the Book of Revelation.

As most religions have been waiting for the Anti-Christ to appear, let it be known that the Anti-Christ is not just with one person. It is about your mind of perception and your ego taken up as your Cain consciousness, a consciousness that is willing to play with the dark and light to learn the wisdom behind your choices and that of dual-energy (good and evil). Where else could your Christ consciousness hide the wisdom of the beast and the Anti-Christ but within your own mental and ego consciousness? And when we decided to exercise our divine plan eons ago, whether as an individual, organization, or collective group, all influences became the work of our biased and judgmental ego-personality of a Cain consciousness that eventually became known as the beast on earth, taken up as mankind.

By reading my books, "The Forgotten Wisdom Behind Genesis Story of Creation" and "The Ascended Masters on the Apocalypse," I have laid out the wisdom behind the number of the beast (666) and who the Anti-Christ is for your study and understanding. All that's left for you to do is research and do your homework because your life and soul depend on it.

From this shallow Cain ego-personality found in mankind today, it shapes this dual-energy (positive and negative) in taking a spiritual course where the belief in power controls all that we are not in spirit. Thus, religion's traditional teachings about us being kicked out of the Garden for disobeying God are based on the perception of sin and not about choice. Therefore, the real story behind the "fall in consciousness" was "choice" and not "sin."

It was placed before us to remain with the "whole of what is our Christ consciousness" or move into the unknown principles of a "three-dimensional consciousness" that took on the belief in power and a God that is outside of us. And, as depicted in the story of creation, most of us chose the "tree of knowledge of good and evil." However, please understand, it does not mean that you sinned or did something wrong or evil. Jesus and the Ascended Masters call it the "choice to experience the opposite to what you truly are at your very core."

The story is symbolic, meaning that we spirits separated ourselves from our Christ consciousness in favor of a mental and physical consciousness that resulted in us forgetting (like death) our divine plan to know "all that there is to know" about dual-energy. What religion defines as sin and death are not about sin and death but rather about a self-induced isolation from being aware that one is Christ, the Goddess, and the source of one's creations, both positive and negative. And when you awaken to this truth, you will work with Crystalline Energy, leaving out all distortions tied to power and control.

If your ego and mind had retained the wisdom of you being Christ, God of Light, and the Goddess, and carried out the divine plan idealized in that wisdom, you would have created a balanced spirit, mind-soul, and ego personalities (lifetimes) in seeing them as not being separate from you. Instead of following through with the concept of your three levels of consciousness as "one body of consciousness," you undertook a great desire to experience and feel your creations first hand using belief systems and your Cain consciousness as the tool to experience opposite roles, light and dark.

This allowed you to descend into a consciousness of power and control that made you believe and feel separate from your Christ consciousness and to all that you are in creation, a sovereign Christ in your own right. And the only way to accomplish this was for your Cain consciousness of immorality to lose sight of your Abel consciousness of awareness of being a Christ also.

The story of Adam, Eve, and the serpent in the Garden is symbolic of that fall and not to be taken literally but as a way for us to grow in consciousness, learn truth over deception, and become awakened. Religion teaches us that we must follow the "will of God," and at the same time, they are teaching us to give away our free will to someone outside of us, which then frightens us and causes much anxiety. Of course, religion knows this, so they continue this teaching of fear because it allows them to steal our energy and power, thus controlling us through our belief systems and using our emotions against us.

Know that the ego-personality aspect that you work out in physical form, no matter if male or female, comes from the emotional part of your feminine nature rather than from your masculine, which explains why the male species feel more important than the female. And, this is also why religions look at women as beneath them. It is the same way in describing many of those that live in the dark today that work out of their Cain consciousness, believing they are the ones to inherit the earth, and we unsophisticated humans are to be their servants and their slaves.

When Jesus walked the earth over two thousand years ago, his ego-personality was named Yeshua Ben Joseph, but later changed by the Kings and the Churches of the world to the name Jesus. Thus, owning the name "Christ" to fool the people to follow them and their narrative of Christ. That is when Jesus became known as "the son of man," then later, after Jesus' baptism, the church called him "the Son of God." However, what the church did not see in this perception of truth, is that the angels of high used this deception and symbolically used the religious story as the "son of man" working out of an unawakened "ego-personality" until such a time mankind awakens to one not only being the "Son of God," but as God, the "Goddess," and a "Christ" simultaneously while in the flesh.

And since one's ego (Cain Principle) is asleep to whom he/she truly is, then they see the "son of man" as someone outside of them. However, the "baptism" of Jesus is symbolic of our mind and ego Cain consciousness coming into the realization that we are playing in duality. Thereby, awakening us to become aware that we are a God, a Christ, and a Goddess. Jesus was the example, showing us how he allowed all parts and pieces of his multidimensional consciousness to become "one again with his Christ consciousness," eliminating all fear that we are separated from our divine spirit.

It is about allowing your Christ spirit, mind-soul, and ego personalities of your past and present lifetimes to become one again, along with using Crystalline Energy in your creations instead of using Earth's dual-energy as the source. Therefore, once your mind-soul (Anti-Christ) and your ego (Cain) consciousness become awakened to this truth, it is then transformed from being the Anti-Christ to becoming the Son of God, then becoming God and the Goddess that is fully aware of your Christhood.

The belief that the male is more esteemed than the female and that there is a God above you filled with power is a big reason we have wars, illnesses, pain, hate, jealousy, rape, and sadness in our earthly experiences. Why? It's because of our male side of self getting into power struggles with our many Cain ego-personalities of the past and with our feminine side of the mind (soul) using that distorted energy by feeding it back to the mind to allow it to manifest our choices as either good or bad and yet, everything is one, neutral, and divine.

With the continuation of our Cain ego-personality acting like a beast (devil), we continuously deceive our male side of the mind (the Anti-Christ) into believing the female side of our mind is to blame for getting kicked out of the Garden (higher consciousness) because of sin (apple). Of course, this is far from the truth! Due to the strong belief in sin, our male side of the mind (Anti-Christ) continues to dump all of our light and dark creations into the female side of our mind (soul) without taking full responsibility for it. And to make matters worse, our Cain ego-personalities of many continue to deceive our male side of the mind into believing that God, power, and the devil are separate from us. Therefore, we need to be saved by someone outside of ourselves.

For example, our politicians, the church, the media, and all those that believe they know what is best for us know that our Cain ego-personality was born from out of our mental mind (the male side) and that of our soul consciousness of responsibility (the female side), and it remains today that our Cain ego consciousness has no authority (power) to make choices. But because of our ego's cunningness, it has our mind-soul persuaded that all power belongs to those egotistical scholars, elites, and people that look at us as their food (energy).

Therefore, that part of our consciousness (Cain) was created as the consciousness that must incarnate into physical form rather than our mind-soul to engage in physical form to learn the wisdom behind our choices. And this is the meaning of Cain getting kicked out of the Garden. And that is when our Cain consciousness became known as the serpent/beast/devil that used persuasion and the killing of our higher awareness (Abel) as the means to motivate our mind-soul (Adam-Eve) into activating many life potentials, beliefs of questionable means, and ego-personalities for us to experience life in such a way to answer the question, "Who am I?"

Hence, our ego (the Cain principle), even though it does not seem that way, ended up becoming a grand friend to our Christ consciousness because it takes our physical ego-personality (beast) to work with our mind-soul (Anti-Christ) to eventually awaken us to the

Christ to whom we are at our core. And since our Christ consciousness is unconditional and forever forgiving, this has become Cain's method to redeem himself for the killing of his higher awareness, symbolized as his brother Abel.

For example, many of us associate Satan as the opposite of God and the devil representing "hell" and God representing "heaven!" And when we speak the name of the Devil, either to ourselves or the name out loud, we feel fear. Why is that? The name itself is tied to many evil acts and effects that we created, see, and experience every day of our lives. Therefore, just in the name itself, we can stir up many underlying emotions deep within, which is why we need to look at the devil as representing "Archangel Lucifer" to get its meaning.

In other words, the name "Lucifer" is found in the Book of Isaiah 14:12 in the New American Bible. *"How have you fallen from heavens, O morning star, son of the dawn. How are you cut down to the ground, you who mowed down the nations?"* As we can see between the older Bible version and the New American Bible, the name "Lucifer" was completely left out, and the words "son of dawn" were added.

In the old testament days, the name "Lucifer" was seen by scholars as a spiritual ruler, like Jesus, that appeared in heaven before God threw him out for disobedience. In 2 Peter 1:19, the Latin word for "Lucifer" refers to the "Morning Star" and having no relationship to the Devil. It was only in post "New Testament" times that the Latin word "Lucifer" was used as the Hebrew name "Sheol," meaning the "Devil."

Because of the misinterpretation and misunderstanding of Archangel Lucifer's name, we became trapped into believing that there is an evil spirit unto himself manipulating our soul and our consciousness in an effort to steal our energy and soul by making us out to be sinners. Well, in the most real sense of the name Lucifer, and how we interpret the name as the Devil, the truth of it all is that Archangel Lucifer is one of the 144,000 angelic families that belong to the Order of the Arc.

Of course, this means, since Lucifer is an Archangel, he, as all Archangels, is an archetypical angel whose name was changed to Satan/Devil for no apparent reason. Therefore, Archangel Lucifer, or to whom we all call the Devil, is the "bearer of light," the "son of the morning," and the "day star," and not Jesus, for Jesus is the angel that helps us work with our own Christ consciousness once the "bearer of light" (Lucifer-Devil) awakens us to it. Hence, the truth is that Archangel Lucifer (symbolized by our Cain ego consciousness) and Jesus (symbolized by our own Christ spirit) are working together for our benefit since the beginning of us coming to earth in the flesh.

In other words, Archangel Lucifer, symbolized by the devil-beast-Cain consciousness, has no mission or assignment to steal our soul or pour down upon us any evil misgivings. He is there to help us, on a physical and mental level, to become aware of our own created demons because we, each of us, are the creator of our reality. And this is why there is no Devil or evil spirit to be afraid of, other than the Devil we created within ourselves and outside of ourselves to fear as if real, just like there is no God outside of us to fear because of sin.

Archangel Lucifer eons ago, before we souled beings entered the earth, was entrusted and appointed by the Order of the Arc to shift our energy and consciousness of duality, positive and negative, light and dark, and our misunderstanding of its nature, back to its "original form of balance." In other words, the redemption of Cain! However, before Archangel Lucifer can accomplish his task, he had to have us believe we took a plunge (fall) in consciousness to an "ego-Cain-personality of deceit, trickery, and perception." And he did it by taking on the role of playing the opposite of Jesus, the Christ. In other words, good versus evil, or darkness (Cain) versus awareness in light (Abel).

This action caused us to feel emotionally that we, too, had fallen, and therefore sinned against God. Thus, Archangel Lucifer, symbolized as our Cain consciousness, became branded as the angel of death, darkness, and the creator of evil. And yet, Lucifer (Cain) is neither, for he is an angel of light that helps us eventually bring in our wisdom of truth as to us souls playing out our choices on earth under the perception that good and evil, light and dark are real.

Since our Christ consciousness is synonymous with Jesus being our savior because of the actions of our ego (beast), Archangel Lucifer, who Cain symbolizes, became the "bearer of light" and the "morning star" for mankind until the Christ consciousness within us is once again awakened and remembered (resurrected). And, when we are awakened to this, it will not seem that bad after all. Through time and space, incarnation after incarnation, opposite forces, positive and negative, good and bad, became the means to how we learned the wisdom behind our choices and how we lacked the understanding of our many ego personalities where they played out in many lifetimes.

And the reason Jesus took on the appearance as a male persona was to convey to the masculine side of our mind that it is indeed the creator of our demon acts to learn the wisdom behind our egotistical choices; simultaneously, to learn "who we truly are" at our core level by playing the opposite of our own divinity. This is also why we can forgive our own Cainable sins because, truthfully, we are Christ, God, and the Goddess who can forgive sins. Why? Because they are not sins, they are experiences chosen by us to learn wisdom. How can wisdom be interpreted as sin?

By Archangel Lucifer doing his job in challenging us to face our demons (dark side) through our ego-personality aspects in the flesh tied to many lifetimes and through other people we associate with, we do become closer to our Christ consciousness with each lifetime. So, rather than trying to disown our dark creations, embrace them because that is where we will find our divinity.

Once we journey through many lifetimes in a three-dimensional consciousness, signified by the third day, we will "rise for a second time from our sleep (dead) state" and move into our Christ state where our ego-consciousness of defiance (Cain Principle) fully ascends (raptures) to a higher state of consciousness (fifth dimension and higher) that ends up leading the "human ego" back into the oneness of consciousness once again.

Therefore, there is no message here of fear, love, hate, right, wrong, or sin. It is simply a message saying that it is okay to let go of our old dogmatic beliefs that we have hung onto for so long. Our physical experiences on earth have been the playground for playing out opposite roles, which transforms our demon creations into much higher and wiser consciousness. This is why what seems like people being righteous and faithful to God, many of them are dark and sinister, complete opposites.

Chapter 10

THE FALSE GOD

What does it mean when Jesus and the Ascended Masters speak about this God found in the Bible as a "false God?" They are referring to the perception of us humans believing in a God that commands worship and fellowship based on the philosophy of there being two opposing forces, God and a Devil. Religions maintain and teach about a holy book where this God of good and a Devil of evil addresses mankind having to choose between them. All because of free will! And the difference between the two is one sends us to heaven, and the other sends us to hell forever and ever.

In Genesis 3:5, and I paraphrase here, when the serpent spoke about the moment when we souls ate the forbidden fruit, that is when our eyes would open and that we would be like gods who will know what is good and what is evil. Therefore, as a God, Christ, and a Goddess unto ourselves, we can only know what is good and evil if we choose to experience them in the physical realm and then believe we are less than a God for it to work.

In other words, when we first awakened to our "oneness of consciousness" and this universal neutralized energy of light eons ago, that was the time when we awakened to a deep desire to learn more about "who we are" from a Christ level. Thus, we souls split our "oneness of consciousness" into three parts: (i) one as our Christ consciousness, (ii) another as an inner (sub) and outer mental consciousness, and (iii) an outer ego physical consciousness to experience our free will to choose. And when we souls, acting as the Spirit of One, simultaneously created energy to match that split consciousness called positive and negative, that is when the "tree of knowledge of good and evil" became known to us as something we could sustain ourselves to a life of soul growth and learning wisdom. And, in the end, we could learn how to be a better and much wiser God-Goddess than before the splitting of our consciousness and the entering of earth.

The Christ part is always neutralized, having no dualness to it, and it is the side of us that cannot ever change as our core essence is unconditional. The inner (Eve) and outer (Adam) mental side of our layered (second) consciousness have become symbolic of the feminine, negative soul side of the mind, and the outer masculine, positive (Adam) side of that same mind that has become the agent that makes choices. The outer ego side, or the third level of consciousness, is known as the experiencer, or a lifetime in a physical body. It is the feminine soul side of one's mind that holds the memories of one's choices made by the masculine side, which is why Adam and Eve became one, as described in the Bible, and which is why "bone of my bone" represents energy mimics energy, and "flesh of my flesh" means consciousness comes from consciousness (Genesis 2:23).

In other words, one's own spirit, the Christ within, essentially created a consciousness of clones of itself. And these clones, one's mind-soul mental and one's ego physical consciousness, are both illusionary. And through these cloned consciousnesses, we ended up using opposing energy to create as many potentials and belief patterns to play out, physically and non-physically. This allowed us to experience life in the flesh for soul growth and learn the wisdom behind our choices. Thus, in effect, the idea of us souls getting kicked out of the Garden for disobeying God is just symbolic of us creating billions and billions of positive (good) and negative (bad) potentials and beliefs for us to experience in the flesh to answer the question, "Who am I?"

We souled beings, the Christ that we are, chose to take a big bite into this cloning of our consciousness, and with using dual-energy to create for ourselves, as many potentials and belief patterns filled with opposing ideas and potentials to experience. This creation allowed us to experience the dark and the light because, in the end, it would deliver to our Christ consciousness (real self) the wisdom behind all those experiences. So, how can we call that sin? However, the only sin that we created was that we all failed to take responsibility for what we created.

By living and creating many clones of self, we just kept on creating as many light and dark creations as possible without giving any thought about the consequences. The more we used this dual-energy in our creations, the more we entered into the unknown effects (abyss) of its consequences. And that is when we all entered into a consciousness belief that it was real because it felt real, all because of the belief in sin.

It was through the creation of dual-energy, positive and negative, which was unknown to us in the beginning stages of our soul development, where our Christ consciousness allowed us to focus out of these clones conscious parts of us and its dual-energy tied to them because of the great desire to know "who we are." My friends, that is and was our purpose! And you thought it was to make it to heaven to live in a utopian setting.

Of course, as time moved forward, our ego-personality, known as the serpent in the Garden, ended up persuading the emotional side of our mind, the feminine, in deciding what energy frequency (neutral, crystal, cosmic, or earth energy) to use for our creations. Yet, one thing was for sure, our masculine side of the mind was the final choice maker and not our Christ spirit or ego. So, in a roundabout way, when religions say the only way to the Father is through the Son, it becomes partially correct. However, they fail to tell you that the Son is symbolic of our mind (the masculine) in using a God energy of duality for our creations.

The idea of your Christ spirit splitting itself into a three-dimensional consciousness was a way for you to devise a "divine plan" to deny your Christ consciousness because it was the only way to grow, learn, and know all things about dual-energy (tree of knowledge of good and evil). And at the same time, you had to forget that you are divine for a while before the plan could be successful. Therefore, you (us souls) did it purposely, and not that some God kicked you out of a Garden. You chose to move beyond your Christ consciousness and this neutralized energy and into this unfamiliar dual-energy to learn what it is like to be God.

Remember Genesis 3:5 again! We would be like gods who will know what is good and evil. Why would we know what is good and evil if we were not already the God that created it all? We are the Goddess who created God in four different energy forms to learn the wisdom behind all that is good and evil, as it was unknown to us at the time. It was about moving into our mental consciousness using Crystalline, Crystal, Cosmic, and Earth energy to experience neutrality or opposites on a scale of losing ourselves in such denseness that we lost our connection to our Christ consciousness in the process. And we did it by pretending we souled beings were not the creator Goddess in sculpturing our reality. And, here we are today, having forgotten that we are the sculptor (the Goddess).

When we lost our awareness of being God, the Goddess, and the Christ having a consciousness of no change and unconditional love and having an energy of neutrality, that is when chaos and confusion played a big part in our mental expressions when it came to our belief systems, especially the belief in good versus evil, right versus wrong, male versus female, religion versus religion, race versus race, heaven versus hell, Democrats versus Republicans, freedom versus confinement, brown eyes versus blue eyes, opposites, that eventually showed up in our physical creations as feeling real.

As you can see, we souls worked hard to hide our Christ consciousness because, otherwise, if our creations became tough or too challenging, we would simply move our focus back into our Christ consciousness without experiencing our choices. Thus, no wisdom could be gained! My friends, it was our own Christ consciousness that sparked the confusion and the chaos that we feel today by having us believe in a false God that presents itself as good and loving, yet in the end, it is still duality. And if we do not worship this false God, then we are destined to follow a Satan character that is bad and non-loving.

From the mind level, when we express a choice to be manifested, good or bad, the first thing we do is receive an impulse coming from our neutralized Christ consciousness. But because of our sleep or unawareness in the flesh about who we are at our core, our beliefs materialize that expression of unawareness using Earth energy and its equivalent frequency, which is the most dualistic and dense energy ever created. And this is why we suffer so much!

This, my friends, is what Jesus and the Ascended Masters are speaking about, as this dual-energy is the false God we have adopted as our creator and savior instead of our own Christ consciousness. It is that simple! And because of our strong belief in this false god (dual-energy), we committed ourselves to turn away from our neutralized energy of light (the real God-Goddess within) in favor of a dual-energy that spins and spirals upward that results in us creating many opposite facets of this dual-energy (false God) to experience.

However, this is not good or bad because it allowed us, by way of our ego-personality, to feel our individuality that eventually has led to shaping this dual-energy and our consciousness more in a denser form, known as our physical body, to grow in spirit and to learn wisdom. And that is when we souls layered our neutralized consciousness into having many types of cloned bodies and consciousnesses, male and female, to experience as light and dark. We can all see this happening around us today, just by paying attention to our politicians and the media of propaganda.

Our physical body's denseness was chosen because it could hold our Christ consciousness to isolate it from our many cloned false light and dark creations. This isolation then allowed us to learn, grow, and evolve through many different lifetimes playing with dual-energy that creates opposites without any interference from our Christ consciousness. As I mentioned before, we did not fall from grace or were kicked out of the Garden (higher consciousness). Instead, we created belief systems (seed) and many-layered consciousnesses about some God kicking us out of the Garden that defines our reality as something real. And yet, it is all an illusion!

Every idea, suggestion, and thought that we have accepted from our religions about God, the serpent, and the Garden, is nothing but a hypnotic state caused by fear and our belief in this false dual-energy of a God to worship as something real. And this is why today, we all maintain the sincerity of a reality we perceive as ours, and yet, all of it is nothing more than a perception on our part.

It is for us to awaken to the truth that it was from a higher consciousness part of us, and not from some God above us, that gave the blessing for our endeavors to experience the many facets of this layered dual-energy. And this is why there is no such thing as sin – for there is no evil, karma, death, or punishment from the spiritual point of view. It is just the belief in these things and karma that makes it feel real. The connection to our own Christ consciousness remains pure at this very moment, and all that we have to do is awaken to it and allow it to come into our lives.

However, because of being asleep to whom we truly are at our core, our Christ consciousness will remain silent until the proper time when we are ready to open our eyes to see and have the ears to listen to what is around us. That is when our Christ spirit will send an impulse to our clone ego-personality to awaken and pass the stolen authority back to the Son (our Mind) to make the right choices. And that is when our Christ consciousness will come forward, guiding us and our clones back to the original state of oneness and pure consciousness and energy.

Do any of you recall the story of Jesus when he was in the desert confronting the Devil? The story tells us that he overcame his Ego and that of this false God (layered dual-energy) and his belief in it. Hence, he gained back his authority as a Christ, and this is why Jesus was more Christ-like after that encounter with himself. And that is when he began to inform his brothers and sisters by saying that "the only way to the Father (pure energy of light) is through the Son (our mind), John 14:6." And now, it is time for us to do the same. But instead, we worship the man and then pay no attention to what he represented as Christ.

The desert symbolizes our multiple layers of ego consciousnesses (clones) that need to come together as "one body of consciousness" taken up as one's Christ consciousness. The Devil is a symbol identifying our ego-personality, refusing to take responsibility for partaking in a force that seems good and evil but, in truth, is neutral. And therefore, we need to become one with our mind-soul, ego, and Christ consciousness before we can understand the question, "Who am I"?

As long as our understanding of God and Satan is based on a religious definition of two separate entities or dual forces, one good and the other bad, our ego and perceptional mind will always be traumatized by our emotional ties, not only to family and friends but to our belief systems. The unpardonable sin taught by religion is nothing more than mankind remaining in ignorance because of our strong emotional ties to our physical family, our stuck beliefs, and our religious rituals. The more we practice our religious rituals, the longer we will be in the dark. The light of truth only comes to us when we let religion, and all that is material, go. For all that is real is within the self.

Remember, our ego will always interfere and judge our choices according to our emotional ties to our beliefs until we awaken enough to change them, our traditions, what family represents to us, and what religions teach as their rituals. It becomes virtually impossible for us to tap into our soul memories about other lifetimes if we keep on allowing our schools, friends, religions, politicians, the media, and family history teach us about God and his dualistic ways as being the truth.

Our Christ consciousness was the gateway through which we came forth from the invisible to the visible, and it is through the invisible, we can come to know the truth and nothing but the truth to whom we truly are.

Chapter 11

RELIGION

What do we know about religion as a whole, other than its teachings of a God that loves power, control, and demands to attend? Everything presented by religion has been the study of a philosophy to create a culture to alleviate the fear of death, save our soul, and a state of fellowship with God that must be without sin. Also, most will follow a religion or a person that can assure some definition about "our creation as a human, why are we here on earth, where do we go when we die, and will we reunite with our loved ones after death?"

Answering these questions means that an average person will adapt to a certain belief in a religion that makes them feel confident, not alone, and that a mystical godlike being will save them after death. And this is why most religions program us to feel worthless, that we are a sinner at birth, and that we have no power to save ourselves, which is why people will flock toward worshipping a mystical God that really is the Devil out of fear more than out of love for truth. It is teachings like this by religion that create a belief where we are convinced that we need a savior.

This type of influence on what we should believe about a savior has us feel that we are not infinite and a sovereign being, creating an emotional mindset where we will always fall short of any perfection under God's eyes. People follow religion blinded by their feelings of unworthiness, shame, guilt, and the fear of God. Thereby they overlook the importance that religion is not good for our health, happiness, and security.

For instance, we often experience depression, anxiety, and other psychological discomforts when it comes to life struggles. And when we are confronted with these symptoms, we usually move to prayer and the giving of money to the church. And if the prayer is not answered in a certain expectation, it causes us to believe that God is not so forgiving as religions proclaim. Therefore, we may deal with ourselves more harshly than one that believes that God is very forgiving.

A good example is when one takes on a strong belief in a merciful God, one will usually experience slower disease progression. But when one believes that God is a punishing God, as taught by religion, one's disease will actually progress faster. Therefore, do we really need to focus all of our attention on religion or learn to do self-research to find our place with truth and the real God? Of course, many could argue that religion does help with our mortality concerns and that they try to keep us respectable with our moral issues.

One could also argue that religion explains the origin of where we came from and who created us but only up to a certain point, and that is where they go blank by saying, "Trust God." But what they are really saying is, "Trust them." However, one could also take the opposite side of most arguments regarding church teachings because most people are uninformed and do not understand God's workings, especially how God and energy work together as one. Therefore, there could be many arguments against religion even being in our lives.

For example, we do not know how Religion became the source for God's word, other than through what the world's scholars have taught us about God's prophets. Remember, it was not that the prophets spoke to them or us directly. It has always been the world's scholars who interpreted their words because, in the old days, when we first wondered about who created us, it was those who could read and understand things on an intellectual level that taught the less fortunate, which was most of the population at the time. And of course, this type of teaching can open us to vulnerability when it comes to power and the control of our minds through brainwashing.

Religion declares that the God of the Bible is the one true God, is very powerful, absolute, is everywhere at once, knows all things, and that God judges only those that fall short in obeying his laws. With this kind of portrayal of God by Religion, it sets us up to feel guilty, feel scared, feel alone, and feel ashamed if we do not follow this God. Thus, mind-control and the taking away of free will happens! And this is what happened to all of us here on earth eons ago, and it still happens today.

We all have been played by the dark forces that live within our religions ever since religion began thousands and thousands of years ago. And they did it by portraying themselves as the gatekeeper and interpreter of God's words, placing power and vulnerability where one becomes exposed to engaging dominion over others, and therefore, the intermediary and the arbitrator for truth. Therefore, as we can understand this kind of portrayal of truth, all of it is fully based on a mind of an intellect that believes in power and control over others. And to achieve this, they use fear! And fear is what the dark forces are all about.

Just look at religion, our politicians, and the media today and how they work hard to keep us in fear. And in doing so, they steal our energy, our thought patterns and have us do what they feel is best for them and not us as mankind. In other words, we all are playing in the hands of the dark forces (the devil), and we do it because of following a God that lives in a Bible claimed to be Holy and true. My friends, all religions on earth, and their scholarly leaders follow a God of darkness, and we, the people, follow them without question.

Why? Because of all those people that are tied to a three-dimensional consciousness, the frequency fluctuates at a level where it can be interfered with by those of the dark forces. It takes one's energy frequency signature and consciousness (DNA) to be at a fifth-dimensional consciousness and higher before one can experience truth, health, and happiness.

Let's use the mask again as an example: The elite, including religion, the media, our politicians, and the so-called professionals that work behind the scenes for our politicians, convince us to wear a mask due to a worldwide virus that is dangerous to us and our loved ones.

Thereby, we need to take responsibility and wear the mask to save our grandfather-mother and those that are most vulnerable to respiratory problems. This is duality and three-dimensional consciousness at its best, as this creates much fear within us where it makes us feel guilty and ashamed if we don't wear the mask.

Thus, they just stole our energy (power), and at the same time, they keep our energy frequency based on a three-dimensional consciousness. Remember, all that is three-dimensional can be interfered with by others. This is mind control, and if we cannot see this, then we are very much asleep and dead to the real God. Know, and understand the symbolic meaning behind wearing a mask. It is to hide from us the truth and how they use fear to keep the truth from surfacing.

Since the beginning of this virus, no one even bothered to ask science or our governments to prove that mask-wearing would even protect us from others and our families. Instead, we just believed in the media and what they proclaimed as truth. For the media, the elites, and those who want us to follow the dark forces (the devil), it becomes easy for them to control our thoughts, beliefs, and actions by using our emotions as a weapon against us.

Today, most of the world population can read, and therefore, these intermediary and the arbitrator for truth want to maintain their power and control over us. And the only way they can do it is to keep fear alive through brainwashing. Remember, a true and loving God works unconditionally and without any fear-based teachings. Jesus himself taught unconditional love, and never did he condemn anyone to hell because of their works, nor did he try to control them by his interpretations of God's words.

In other words, the more we are kept in fear and emotionally tied to guilt and shame, the more controllable we are, thus, fulfilling our oppressor's needs as we become their slaves and source for their creations and not ours. And we thought slavery was something of the past! According to Jesus' channeled messages, most of the world's population is under mind control because of our emotions. Therefore, we are under the control of the dark forces (the devil).

If we could open our minds and do some research beyond the intellect and what we have been taught by our parents, our friends, our religion, science, and our schools, we would find that God does not work in the way of duality and discord. God works through the living! We have forgotten that life itself is infinite and not limited only to whom we think we are from a dualistic and intellectual level. You are infinite and an absolute creator of your experiences, and you should never doubt that your consciousness is, in fact, the Goddess you seek. The "I exist" in consciousness is all about you and how "you can create and be anything you want to be" because you are the creator of your world.

My identity and your identity are not fixed only to what we experience through consciousness but are all about what we "act on in consciousness," no matter what dimension we work from, and the dark forces know this, which is why they work hard to keep us from raising our DNA frequency above a three-dimensional consciousness. It comes to understanding that consciousness is not a single expression or dimension because that is not reality. It is that we have come to believe it as our reality. Our mind says it has to be our reality and our truth, but what we think is our reality, really isn't.

In other words, if "I exist," as in consciousness only, and my physical body is a byproduct of my consciousness, then I can choose what I want to believe, disbelieve, and experience for my reality. And if I choose to believe COVID-19 is real, then it becomes real, and so does the mask-wearing in facing our fears. But if I choose not to believe in its reality, then how can I ever contract the disease? Why do I say this? Because layered energy always responds to consciousness!

For example, if my consciousness is vibrating at a much higher frequency, like, for instance, a fifth-dimensional consciousness, then COVID-19 becomes impossible to activate the disease within me or me passing it on to anyone else. However, since we souls, together, are the creator of layered energy (God) and the Goddess we seek, then what we believe as our truths in this three-dimensional world, the energy surrounding that truth has to respond to what we as a group, believe. If we as a group consciousness let go of the fear in COVID-19, then the layered energy surrounding it changes to where it disappears.

But if we, as a group, fear the virus, then COVID-19 becomes part of our three-dimensional reality where one can catch the virus even though taking a vaccine. Suppose most of the human consciousness believes a shot will clear up the disease. Still, only a few take the shot because of their emotional ties to family, friends, and their religion. Out of nowhere, the disease could disappear because of the energy of human consciousness changed around the belief in it.

However, suppose one takes the shot because of their emotional ties to a belief one is still in control of one's life due to their spiritual understanding. In this case, one is fooling oneself because one is still working out of fear because of the emotional ties to the virus's dual-energy rules. Therefore, since one's emotions are still tied to a three-dimensional consciousness belief, one can still contract the virus.

As humans, living in a world of mass consciousness belief in dual-energy as our savior, we lose control of what we want to experience by adding to the frequency of what we are trying to prevent. Suppose we are bombarded, day after day, by our religious beliefs, our politicians, and emotional ties to family, friends, and the media about what is right and what isn't. Then, by all means, in this case, we will create the reality they want for us to experience and not what we want to experience. All because of us adding energy to what they wanted for us to experience, we end up living in their reality because we helped them create it through believing in their propaganda.

We know this to be true just by these dark forces taking more and more of our freedoms away until, before we know it, we live in a society where our leaders keep us from what we want to do. In other words, we become blind to the dark forces and how they are acting as our God and Savior, not realizing they are stealing our energy to create their reality and not ours. An excellent example of this is that we have a constitutional right to free speech and assembly, and yet our free will and our freedom to breathe have been taken away from us by those in power.

Also, keep in mind that if we remain asleep to the dark forces and how they portray God and the Bible as something holy and true, then what we experience in life depends on what energy frequency we are dialed into. And if we are locked into a consciousness controlled by our emotions, then that is the energy used by our consciousness and others in creating the world in what we do not want. We live in a multi-dimensional world, and there are many of us on earth that vibrate at many different frequencies, thus many different consciousnesses.

Thereby, by sight and feelings alone, one that is not emotionally controlled, will always work from a higher frequency where one can witness many different realities and experiences of others here on earth. Those that function at a lower frequency level do not even realize that we are watching them play in an energy of disorder. And the more we try to awaken them to this, the more they fight against the light and feed the dark. This is where compassion comes in and then allow those that are still asleep to learn by themselves.

How long will it take you to realize that there is more going on right in front of you than what you see and what you are being told by our media, our religions, and our governments? Yes, we all have a passion for enlightenment, but many love working with the dark side without them even knowing they are doing it. They think, believe, and trust that they are doing God's work by having compassion, and yet, that compassion is emotionally controlled by others. And this is why, from the ascended master's point of view, it is found on a conditional mindset that religion, their false god, and our emotions have all become the tool for distraction for the dark side. However, it is not all bad because, as I mentioned before, it was the only way to become awakened to our own Christ consciousness and to learn the wisdom behind what is right and what is considered evil.

My friends, enlightenment is not about what we think it is from a spiritual level or about getting more comfortable because we follow the Bible and go to church. It is about realizing and becoming awakened to a knowing that everything there is to know about life, dual-energy, feeling free, that you are Christ in the flesh, and that this God of the Bible is not who you believe him to be. Why? Because religion and the dark forces own this God of the Bible, for they are the ones that created him. Why do I say this?

It is because I have learned that enlightenment is the integration of one's many ego-personality clones from many different lifetime experiences. Thereby, raising one's vibrational frequency signature (DNA) to a higher frequency where one can observe more than what a three-dimensional person is observing from a three-dimensional world. And this integration and observation come when we learn to accept ourselves as more than just a human here on earth and not as someone seeking to be saved by religion or some force, we call God, or Jesus coming from out behind some cloud, or a person, group, or organization that knows more.

Remember, all religions and their philosophies about a God of good and evil come from an unawakened individual filled with fear, emotional conflict, persuasion, judgment, and pride, all designed to control all aspects of their consciousness. Thus, leaving them locked into a consciousness and a state of mind that is very limiting, as one's mind becomes blind to only what it has been taught and subject to in its frequency when it comes to truth and awareness of spirit.

Therefore, religion, governments, and the media love to work with our ego and an unawakened mind (symbolized by the beast and the Anti-Christ) because it keeps them in power and in control of our consciousness, mind-soul, our energy, and our ego clones of many (personality aspects) that are spread throughout numerous dimensions. And they use everything holy, emotionally, and giveaways as a smokescreen to maintain that power and control over us, including having us feel guilty, ashamed and that we should never question them, their God, or religion.

Our politicians, big businesses, Hollywood, professional sports, and the media are in the same boat as our religions, as they all work together to keep us in fear and asleep to whom we truly are as a Christ in our own right. And, since the "beast" and the "Anti-Christ" works for the dark forces, then one could say that these organizations all work for the devil, including this God of the Bible and who supports it.

When we accept ourselves as a Christ, a God, and a Goddess, then all parts and pieces of our consciousness (the clones) that are spread throughout the many-dimensional realms will find their way back home to our human memory of today, where we can begin to open up consciously to "all that we are as a Christ and not as an emotional defeatist." Thus, feeling fulfilled and complete rather than feeling like pieces of a puzzle spread out and alone. And once we feel this completion, it is not so much about our purpose and the meaning of life anymore but about our many experiences learning to be a "sovereign being (God-Goddess)" in our own right.

From time to time, we must learn to study spiritual things that do not come from an emotional dualistic approach due to our attachments like religion, philosophy, family, friends, the Bible, and its many mysterious workings of a God that is actually part of the dark. As for me, none of them have the answer to what I feel inside. Not the Bible, any religion, family, friends, or any holy book, because all that was written and interpreted for centuries was all done by scholars and family that believe the mind is who we are and what makes up our identity as being a human.

Any person of a church who tries to remind us to worship this God of the Bible then knows not what they are saying because what they need to learn about this God is for them to stop trying to figure him out as far as being our creator and simply consider God as an energy source in manifesting our desires and interest as a Goddess in training. Know that the human ego and the unawakened mind have no concept whatsoever of ascension (rapture) because they simply cannot understand the greater self as a Christ also.

All that the unawakened mind and ego are focused on is survival and its place in the world. And, after death, where does one go, heaven or hell? In fact, an unawakened mind and ego will work hard not to understand the enlightenment of one's soul because they are too busy working with mental behaviors, such as good and evil, survival, and what it feels like emotionally if one let's go of family members and a God that hates and uses everything of holy to cover it up.

We all have forgotten how cunning the dark forces can be when learning about who God, Christ, and self are from a mental understanding. And this is what Jesus experienced over two thousand years ago when he tried to awaken those of the day about who they truly are and who they are not. But only a few listened, and therefore, the mass consciousness in those days crucified him without even realizing they were participating with the Roman Empire and their devilish ways in doing things. And it would be the same today, as Christians worldwide would not recognize Christ, only a few, and therefore, crucify Christ again.

Understand that an unawakened ego-personality on its own has no power and, therefore, needs to steal it from others. Of course, the ego (the clone) is very good at persuasion, and therefore, it is not responsible for our ascension, awakening, or enlightenment. That is up to our soul record of responsibility, or the Eve principle. Why is that? It is because our soul carries the memory of what we, from the mind level, chose and lived out in all those cloned lifetimes, past, present, and future.

We need to learn to quiet our mind and do some deep breathing for at least fifteen to thirty minutes a day and allow our soul to feed our mind in having our ego-personality let go of what is not real and allow the wisdom to be passed on to our mind of the intellect for nurturing. And from that nurturing, our mind will one day awaken to the fact that our ascension (rapture) is a very personal process that cannot be taught by anyone of an emotional, intellectual, and reasoning mind, and this includes our religion and their orators, the media, governments, family, and friends.

Why? Because our past stories (lifetimes) are not what we think they were, and the events tied to them did not unfold as our mind remembers them. Our mind only understands those events (stories) as limitations and sin, and not as experiences passed down to our Christ consciousness as wisdom. In fact, because the unawakened mind and ego have distorted views of what happened in past lifetimes, our current life becomes the reality we are experiencing right now because of our beliefs tied to those past lifetimes. And, we thought that we were in charge of our life!

We are not in charge of our life because the energy we bring with us in each lifetime carries its own energy and consciousness, thus its own personality and reality. And when this is not understood from an unawakened mind and consciousness, then the life we have right now becomes very confusing and with suffering. The world, my friends, is getting very loud and messy and out of control, and with it, religions, our politicians, and the media have begun to step up their rhetoric more than ever about the end days, Jesus' return, and that the financial system needs to reset or otherwise we are doomed.

My friends, it is all lies because it is coming from the dark forces and not from those that are awakened to the real truth. There have been many dreams, visions, movies, and books written on the subject of the last days. And all of it was designed and written by the dark forces, including the Book of Revelation, to make us feel frightened, guilty, emotional, and ashamed because of refusing to join the dark forces and their ideas of slavery.

It is not about Jesus' return, the last days, or about Allah as we understand it. It is about religions, politicians, and the media worldwide, confining us into slavery, population reduction, and fear by introducing us to a war of all battles. Jesus and the Ascended Masters feel our fears and hear our prayers because they know that our hearts are troubled by what is taught to us about God, our economy, and how we all can live in freedom.

Religions know that we feel something that indicates the end days, which is why it was the dark forces that took control of the Bible, the God we worship, and how we look upon Christ as our savior. All of it was designed to destroy us when the time was right for the dark forces to trigger it. For example, look at how we worship the man Jesus instead of looking upon his message about the Christ consciousness. We need to learn to celebrate Christ's consciousness and not the man.

However, because of the dark miscalculating mankind's heart, the dark knows and feels that many of us are beginning to awaken to their practice of leading us into more darkness. And because of it, the dark is feeling the intensity of a New Energy moving upon earth that will light up the dark, exposing all the falseness of those taking advantage of us. And this includes our religions, politicians (city, county, state, and federal level), Hollywood, and all those that work hard to take away our sovereignty and freedom.

In fact, this current time span (December 20, 2020) was the beginning when those who use power for self-gain, to harm and destroy, will find themselves exposed to this light faster than ever before in history. And this is why many of us will begin to see our religious scholars, the media, and our politicians going off the deep end and doing extreme acts where they will show their real intent. Why? Because we are moving into the Golden age of sovereignty. Today, it can be seen with the media around the world trying to keep us in darkness because they know that there will be no turning back once the people awaken.

My friends, it is all about learning to trust in your intuition and taking the first step into raising your three-dimensional consciousness to a fifth-dimensional consciousness, or you will find yourself left behind in a world of fear and darkness. It becomes your choice in what dimension you want to experience as your reality. So, take time to deep breathe throughout the day and feel this darkness fighting hard to maintain its power and control over you. The darkness is there in the media, big businesses, your religion, and your politicians as they are beginning to be exposed for their lies, deceitfulness, and schemes to keep you from learning the truth. When doing the deep breathing, feel into how these dark forces have brainwashed you into trusting them as your leaders. It is all there for your viewing!

The virus and the vaccine that we are experiencing today are symbolic of the dark forces to steal our energy to control us. Thus, take off this mask, the false face of your oppressors, and hold true to whom you truly are, a Christ in the workings that knows the answer to the question, "Who am I?" Therefore, take deep breaths and do self-study, and while you are at it, learn to stand behind the short wall and allow those who oppress you to expose themselves right before your very eyes.

Many of us have forgotten about our body, our personality clone consciousnesses, and all that surrounds us is nothing but energy, an energy that comes in as a frequency that can lift us into the fifth dimension and higher where no one can control us ever again. Know that the dark force's greatest weapon is to keep us asleep, emotional, and in ignorance to the truth, as their greatest fear is that we will awaken to them and their system to keep us in slavery.

For example, when the first organized religion began after the death of Jesus over two thousand years ago, religion was much in tune with Jesus' spiritual ideals. However, a few hundred years after his death, religion decided to recruit scholars, intellects, and the elite, to help make us slaves to them through mind control. Even by using Simon Peter as the rock, religion adopted the first pope, then priests, clerics, ministers, and pastors as shepherds to become God's mouthpiece, which is why they had to rid the world of Simon Peter before it could work.

It was then that religion decided that the people needed to be taught what Jesus meant when he spoke of God and the Kingdom, all because in our early stages after Jesus' death, we, the people, did not have the aptitude in comprehending God's workings. Therefore, once the words of Jesus and his disciples were dimmed because of the passing of time, religion changed the narrative regarding how we were introduced to God and Christ.

And now, after generations have passed from Jesus's death, not only did religion take control of our spiritual training, we allowed the elites and our government leaders to take away our sovereignty as a spiritual being and placed it with us having to worship a false god. And now, we are kept locked into a consciousness of darkness and ignorance. When religions used Moses' teachings to a one God concept, this allowed the dark forces to announce that Jesus was the Son of God in the flesh who died for our sins; thus, allowing religion to name Jesus not only as the son of God but also our father, our creator, and our savior.

And once this was accomplished, religions then introduced to us rules to follow, or else we could risk punishment in hell. This also gave religion the needed icon to sell their God of hate, conditional love, fear, and darkness instead of life, light, and truth. And Jesus was that icon because we could relate to him on an emotional level because of him being in the flesh. Now, I am not saying Jesus is of the dark forces. Jesus is of the light, but the dark used his name after his death to benefit them.

Remember, it is always through our emotions where we meet our spiritual destruction. So, wake up before it is too late! Even though during Jesus' life on earth, he never testified that sin was something right or wrong or that he was our God and savior. It was religion that used Jesus, the man, as a ploy to move us away from learning the real message behind his teachings, which was about all of us being a Christ in our own right. And as a group consciousness, we were fooled into believing Christ is something of a name given by God to his Son, not realizing that Christ is consciousness and the acting force within us all that makes us a sovereign Goddess.

Religion's dark forces worldwide led us all down a path filled with pride, lust for power, resentment, laziness, grief, greed, and jealousy as a foundation to experience life and then called it sin. They even changed the name of Jesus because his real name was Yeshua Ben Joseph. And from these teachings that we all accepted as truth, we took on an energy pattern where we followed in the footsteps of our supposed creator, an image of a God of sin and punishment.

And from this strong belief in this god of sin and punishment, we allowed religion to exert its power and control over us by opening the door for kings, rulers, and governments to control all aspects of our lives. By the dark forces eons ago taking control of all religions worldwide, it led to controlling all aspects of our government, from local to the highest. And now, they have completely convinced us that we are not smart or divine enough to understand Jesus, God, Christ, and the ways of the angels.

And therefore, we allowed their shepherds (priests, ministers, etc.) and the politicians to be the go-between in trusting them to protect, feed, and help us with our health and spiritual understanding. When, in fact, they have been feeding us nothing but lies to keep us asleep from ever knowing they are killing us slowly with their patented foods, patented medicines, their vaccines, the mask, and their financial system. However, in today's age and consciousness, new expanded energy is moving in fast throughout the earth where people are beginning to awaken to this take over by the cunningness of the elites and their dark magic in deceiving us.

By paying attention to their words and actions, one can see their controlling and deceptive ways beginning to be evident because we have experienced it firsthand. By using fear and our emotions about how God manages the Law of Obedience, it continues to give religion and the powerful elites what they need to steal our energy (money) and keep our soul and consciousness locked into giving away our sovereignty as a Christ, and also to their dark and egotistical ways.

Because of our laziness or fear to study spirit and ourselves as a Christ also, equal to God and not less than, the dark forces (the devil) found religion and our governments as the means to control everything about us without us realizing we are helping them maintain their power, richness, and control over us. They influence us by telling us who we must vote for as our leaders without realizing we are sanctioning our slavery to the devil and dark forces. And it is not about belonging to one political party or the other, for they are both equally belong to the dark forces.

Know that the world's dark forces love to keep us in fear about what constitutes sin, salvation, or that we are divine, and they know this causes us to feel lost, alone, hurt, and abandoned by God and our governments. To that, Jesus and the ascended masters say, "Fear not, for the time has come for the expanded truth to emerge from the darkness of our consciousness," thus allowing us to see them as to whom they truly are and what they have been up to in keeping us blind to the real truth behind our existence.

All that is left for us to do is to be part of the awakening (harvest) and allow our mind-soul and ego consciousness to shift toward a higher calling than what religion and our governments advocate as truth. Know that the wisdom that I am conveying is about the Christ within us all, disclosing to you that the religions and governments are very dark, abusive, deceptive, distant, conditional, and very cold and calculating when it comes to hiding the truth about who we are on a deeper level. And this is why we must set aside the Bible as we know it today because, for centuries, religions and governments have changed the writings and their meanings, not counting what was left out of the Bible on purpose to fool us; thus, changing the message from the old prophets to a message of fear, control, and power.

Yes, we can honor the Bible and all holy books and thank the old prophets for their messages that somehow made it through. Nevertheless, and this comes from the old prophets, such as Jesus, that it is essential to understand that it was not the material world that came first or the Bible. It was our "Christ Consciousness," and then everything else followed. We have forgotten, because of the belief in time and space, that at one time, we did know that we were God, the Goddess, and Christ, but that knowingness eventually gave way to an ego-personality consciousness that was seized by the Cain Factor that became completely programmed by all that is dark and evil.

At our core level, we know that we are nothing but a consciousness that spirals in an upward movement as the human mind and ego evolve in frequency. Therefore, the real God-Goddess, and the Christ within, is not stagnant, dull, or entirely unknown to us but it is there in its purest absoluteness, waiting for us to reconnect to it on a conscious physical level. Remember, your Christ spirit is without form, structure, size, height, weight, or color, and power because power is just symbolic of your own authority as a God-Goddess.

We all must understand when it comes to power, control, and consciousness, we need to be present and awakened to the truth about being a free sovereign agent of the Spirit of One. Even our reality cannot exist without consciousness because it takes consciousness to draw in this "universal omnipresent neutralized unbiased energy of light (God)" as to how we are to structure and exhibit our reality outward. Therefore, there is no such thing as power or a God of good and evil, other than the illusion of it that makes them real. And as with this good and evil, or the illusion of it, having power over another soul only comes from an unawakened mind that believes physicalness is all that we are in consciousness.

It is our consciousness that configures our energy into what we choose to experience, good, bad, or neutral. Therefore, our choices come from what we believe about what is around us regarding family, friends, the media, our politicians, our religion, and that of a false God, all because of believing in sin, good and evil. The mind judges' power as real without seeing its formulation was actually created by one's own Christ consciousness through the composition of one's own universal omnipresent unbiased energy. Remember, you are the creator of your energy, and what you do with it is up to you.

Through this act, your mind, that of power, and this God of sin and punishment have become a result of your soul perceiving a mental image of a God as being real. And now we know this is not true! Of course, we cannot blame religion for their perception of God because that is just how we designed the system for a three-dimensional planet. It is not that we are some lab rats for God's testing either, but it may be that we, the people that created religion, are blinded by our own greed for power, money, and the controlling of our intentions.

However, regardless if we blame religion or how we feel spiritually, physically, and emotionally, religions will always affirm their rigid teachings as to narrating God as someone to fear. And as long as there is fear, there is submission! And this submission comes with a system designed for us to never question religion and their God and our governments. Because all that does is induce more guilt, shame, and more fear about following their rules, thus leading us to experience more suffering.

For centuries, it has only been our religions that gave notice to what constitutes God's advisors and translators of his written words without realizing they are only one part of the equation that keeps us asleep and unaware of who we truly are at our core. But here I am today, in a new body, where only a few can recognize me. It was the same for John the Baptists, as he was an incarnation of Elijah and Moses an incarnation of Muhammad. Even Jesus, the Christ, was not recognized by religion in his day. And, if Jesus came back today, he still would not be recognized.

And by religion not recognizing and accepting reincarnation as one of the primary avenues to experience all things, good and bad, to become a much wiser God, they can market their false God by keeping us in fear, very emotional, and guilt-ridden. This also allows religion to control our beliefs, thoughts, choices, and actions, which provides them the ingenuity for maintaining their power, influences, and control over us and our salvation.

Because of our fear over salvation, we make it easy for the dark forces within religions and governments to manipulate us by giving them our allegiance, our worship, our money, and our obedience to them and their God that is false. No matter what sin you may think you have committed against the ruling body of any church, in God's eyes, sin is nothing more than you experiencing with your creative consciousness. And, like you, I am more than just what religion believes that I am. I even can declare without any thought of burning in hell that I was a disciple of Jesus when He walked the earth over two thousand years ago.

I cannot prove it by showing some papers. It is that Jesus, the Christ, himself has informed me that I had a lifetime with him, and I played out the role as Simon Peter, his disciple. Not only that, but I also remember Simon Peter, the disciple, because I can feel his personality pulling at me sometimes to be heard. Therefore, I write this chapter about religion, their God, and their Shepherds, as well as Sin, Death, Christ's Return, and Satan, and that we are indeed the real God-Goddess, Christ, and the Son.

This idea comes from Simon Peter's aspect and from Jesus himself along with the Ascended Masters. Therefore, as an ordained disciple, given me by Jesus, the Christ himself, and that of my own "I AM"

Christ consciousness as a "priest under the order of Lord Melchezidek," my purpose is to inform as many people as possible about the second coming of Christ. And, this second coming I speak of is "you" coming into an awakening and learning that the Rapture is nothing more than your "ascension" from a three-dimensional consciousness to a "fifth-dimensional consciousness," where you are awakened as a Christ. However, it must be allowed and accepted!

Allow me to leave you with this! Have you ever asked religion and their Shepherds, or whatever you desire to call them, why their God allows one to be born rich and educated while another born poor and uneducated? Or, why one is born into an abusive family while another into a very loving family? What about those born physically challenged or in a very oppressive regime? Why are some ugly while others beautiful? Why are some born to be six feet seven inches while another four feet seven inches? How about one being born with overwhelming privileges while another is relatively disadvantaged? What sin was committed in all of these circumstances?

Chapter 12

OUR REALITY IS BASED ON LIES

All that we believe as our reality, it is based on perception, judgment, rational thinking, and a faithful system of philosophical concepts describing how we formulate and administer information about how things work around us. Our belief in these things, including God, Satan, our existence, and survival, is what most of us use to develop our personality, integrity, and understanding of the circumstances and conditions bounding us to our truths. However, no matter how we slice reality and its meaning, it is a principle guideline that universally exists outside of our mind that we use to determine our beliefs and truths.

And when we look at the rational mind of a believer in this God of the Bible, Satan, and in their perception of life, and how they judge what truth is or what is a lie, it is all based on logic, right, wrong, and the many unpleasant events that they may have experienced. Thus, forgetting that they are the creator of it all. Now, why is that? It is because of how the rational mind loves to wrap itself around what it doesn't understand about its environment, what is happening to it, and how God and mankind deal with one's emotions under the guise of fairness, salvation, and justice.

It is about our mental and physical senses where we wrap ourselves around our emotions in such a way to make sense of what constitutes a lie or truth. For example, we hear the media, and we look at our religion, our neighbors, friends, the financial system, and our politicians, not just in the United States, but around the world, and how they are all trying to influence us into believing that they know more than we do, especially when it comes to our safety, our spiritual and physical health, and our understanding of the dangers ahead. We listen, and then we adopted their discernment on these matters as our truth.

Of course, there are a few out there that dig a little deeper within their hearts on what they feel, see, hear, and are told about these things. And it seems to them what they are being told to believe is not working in their eyes because it keeps leading them to poverty, pain, and more uneasiness. Just the chaos and confusion they are seeing and feeling around them makes them feel vulnerable and helpless to where they are beginning to question themselves, asking, "What is the real truth?"

Truth, of course, is not about our safety, spiritual and physical health, what is right or wrong, good or bad, or even what we did in life to be sorry for. It is about becoming aware of "who we truly are, and then having the courage to face ourselves" with the real truth over the lies that we all have been taught for centuries by religion, our government, our teachers, the media, our friends, and our family.

My friends know that truth expands as consciousness expands, and therefore what was true yesterday is not the truth today. Jesus and the ascended masters can understand that some of us are afraid to look at our unbending and fixed truths (beliefs) because of how we were brought up as a Democrat, Republican, Catholic, Protestant, or whatever belief we bow down to. Not only that, but we were also brought up to believe that we are black, white, brown, yellow, red, that we are multiple genders, that wrong is wrong, right is right, and with no in-between, and that there is no such thing as reincarnation. That, my friends, is one working out of a consciousness of stagnation, unawareness, and inaction.

Despite all these lies you take as your truths, Jesus and the masters ask you to take a moment and feel into what you perceive as your truths. And when you do, you will find that ninety-nine percent of your truths come from your rational mind and how it has been trained that way for millions of years. Without realizing it, ninety-nine percent of all your life choices actually come from your emotional footprint based on lifetimes past, those that are around you, and not from your current lifetime.

It has also been with your perception of a God that created you, a Satan that is after your soul, and that of mass consciousness reinforcing the use of "Earth Energy" and your mind and physical body as being "all that there is" about you. Because of this hypnotic layering and layering that has been going on in consciousness, lifetime after lifetime, you automatically firmly uphold your truths that nothing can exist beyond your three-dimensional reality and consciousness.

Everything we see, feel, and hear, either as good or bad, right or wrong, up or down, heaven or hell, is directed toward the perception of your mind and how you interpret your environment as to what is real. Therefore, every thought, truth, or belief that you have is likely to take on an emotional response pattern of a mental nature that places you in a situation where the "mind-soul" is all that there is when it comes to determining what is real and unreal, consequently overlooking your Oversoul (the Christ within).

Since your mind operates on a mental hierarchy, it uses Cosmic and Earth Energy as its source for experiencing that hierarchy in the flesh. However, even though it feels that way in the flesh, there is no such hierarchy in truth. Thus, perception becomes your method of discerning your truths, your lies, and who you are. And when your consciousness evolves and expands through time and space, lifetime after lifetime, so does your perception of truth and who you are. Therefore, confirming that "truth" and who you are "expands" as your consciousness expands.

Everything around us and within us spiral upward in a circular motion, all because of cause and effect. Therefore, either outward or inward, what is left behind has to collapse through evolution, including our truths, lies, and who we are. And if you do not accept this explanation, then be prepared to live out more lifetimes until you do. Keep in mind the understanding of karma and why we experience it. Like the blind man that Jesus healed! It didn't come from his current life but a lifetime past.

So, the best way to explain what is happening around us is that the world is not really falling apart because we and the world are merely changing the way we connect to our emotional consciousness. Therefore, it may seem like doomsday because of what is going on around the world. And yet, be assured, the only thing changing is that of the "Four Building Blocks of God (Energy)," transitioning the ego-personality consciousness of our past and present (because of karma), to look beyond what we call our reality and our truths today.

Why? Because in every reality, past or present, there is energy vibrating at many different frequencies. It is that Earth and some of us living upon it are moving into the fifth-dimensional frequency. All of us here on earth made life contracts with our spirit a long time ago, before coming into the flesh, and these contracts were based on how the "four building blocks of God's energy" work. And three out of the four are based on dual vibrational energy and how it affects us on a soul level.

Many of us have had multiple lifetimes playing with this multi-dimensional vibrational energy where we have experienced both male and female, rich and poor, educated and uneducated, brown eyes and blue eyes, and that we experienced all races and creeds. And, in the end, we do come to a point in a lifetime where we pick up a passion for learning the real truth about "who we are, who we are not, and what energy is, compared to what it isn't."

Life contracts can be spotted if one is paying attention. For example, from birth to the present, my life contract gave me the means to go into business three times and experience firsthand the manipulating of truth as I found myself being challenged at all levels of my consciousness. Thereby, I have experienced many levels of energy frequencies. Now, I will not repeat myself from what was already given in the book's early chapters, but I will summarize to get the point.

As said, I was born in 1948, just a few years after World War II, and into a Catholic family, somewhat conventional in terms of traditions, having siblings that are traditionalist as far as their core beliefs; and, at a very young age, I could feel and see spirits around me. Then at the age of twenty-three, married, having four children, I found myself in 1971, acquiring the financial support to enter the business world. However, the company and I filed bankruptcy three and a half years later because of trying times.

Then in early 1975, I unexpectedly saw three Franciscan Monks dressed in their traditional attire emerge from the darkness of my bedroom, giving me a message about learning the real truth in this lifetime. However, because of my passion for business, I again found myself in business in late 1975. But this time, it lasted eighteen years before losing my company once again. However, in 1993, a few months after losing the business for the second time, I again found myself going back into business for the third time. And from 1993 to the year 2000, I moved my company from Pennsylvania to Eastern Tennessee, where my company developed an e-procurement system for the U.S. Air Force Military bases stationed overseas to purchase their vehicle parts.

It was from this location in Tennessee, and the use of our well-established e-procurement system for the military, where the idea was born to develop a new e-procurement system for cities, counties, and state governments that led me to hire a highly educated and persuasive intellect of a person to market it. However, all that came from this person's persuasive personality was about myself going down a path of almost losing my company once again. That is when, in 2004, I found myself and my company in the red for the first time since I opened the doors in 1994. I was nearly broke and just hanging on with a very thin thread.

So, I started praying to the Monks that visited me way back in 1975 and not to some God above me. Then out of nowhere, just before getting out of bed one morning, I was stunned when Jesus himself appeared before me, revealing himself to me in the flesh and then telling me that everything will be fine. Later that morning, I went to work, gathered those folks involved, and closed down the LLC company. I then fired this highly persuasive personality, took the loss, and began to focus on the things that were important to me.

As you can see, my contract for this lifetime was to learn the real truth about "who I am, who I am not," and how energy works by living it out through the many hidden lies that surrounded me. And, in the end, the greatest truth of all, I learned that "I am a Christ in my own right." And that "I am still a disciple of Jesus (Christ)" in this lifetime as I was Simon Peter in that lifetime.

Therefore, what better way for me to learn this truth than to be born a Catholic, my family being penniless, my beliefs different from my siblings, and then meeting and working with people with a personality nature about themselves that ended up challenging me to my very core. It was from the family that I was born into, to the individuals I met and worked with, including the visitations from the monks, to seeing Jesus in my home, that I had to experience the untruths, the deceptions, the lies, and cover-ups, and all that was hidden within my soul memories from past lifetimes to now before I could discover the "truth" that the monks talked about in my vision back in 1975.

It was from this contract I made with my soul before entering earth in 1948 that eventually led me into the study of Biblical Scripture where I learned about how religion, businesses, the media, family, friends, and governments, consciously or unconsciously, presented themselves in an unenlightened and hidden way because the real truth can only come from within oneself when one's consciousness and energy frequency are ready to receive it. Therefore, know that there is no one above you, no God or any high angel, including Archangels, then yourself.

You are it, the creator, the Christ, God, and the Goddess, all rolled up into "one body of consciousness." And it was at that point in my life where I awakened to the meaning of what the Monks meant by their statement telling me back in 1975 that "It was meant for me to learn the truth in this lifetime."

My friends, we have been lied to for a long time, and how we perceive our truths is what creates our reality today. If our truths are all about good and evil, then that is what we will experience as our reality. And as a disciple of Jesus over two thousand years ago, he implanted a new truth within my soul memory, hoping that it will take root one day. And this new truth did take root as it had stayed under the surface of my soul consciousness for about two thousand years before it began to sprout. And today, this truth is in total metamorphosis for me.

Here I am today, born into a new body and environment where I have chosen the reality that set me up as a Christ where I can now take up where I left off as Simon Peter and pass the message down to those of the earth that are ready in consciousness frequency to hear it. And if you are reading this material, then more than likely, you have the energy and consciousness frequency to hear the message. However, does it resonate with you!

So, I ask you to learn to let go and not be a slave to your so-called truths. Be honest with yourself and feel into your consciousness. That is where truth comes forward to set you free from a mind that only operates on a perceptional and emotional level. It is the addictiveness in using dual-energy, positive and negative, as to what keeps you stuck in a revolving cycle that only sees good and evil, right and wrong, light and dark, God and Satan, and yourself as a human in need.

When you learn to trust that you are equal to God, and not less than, equal in all phases of consciousness and frequencies, it allows your emotional mind and consciousness to open up to the totality of "who you truly are at your core," and to your relationship to your soul and intuitive consciousness. That is when your wishes, dreams of health, wealth, and happiness are then at our fingertips. But we give these things away for the mere benefit of holding onto old dogmatic truths, traditions, and the idea of some god in a book is going to come and save us someday, but only if we play by His rules.

Chapter 13

KNOWING THAT YOU ARE CHRIST, GOD, AND A GODDESS

For centuries, we have been taught that we have a soul that can't be understood in an absolute and conclusive way because it cannot be seen or witnessed as real. Religions maintain the idea that as long as we are alive on earth, the soul is with us, but once the body dies, the soul departs; either in heaven, hell, or somewhere in-between. For these reasons, the soul is unpleasantly seen by many as negative more than positive.

Religions also declare that the soul causes the physical body to grow and have animation because, without it, the body would deteriorate and die, which is partially true. However, the Christ spirit (the Goddess-Oversoul) injects the life force into the body, thus animating the brain-mind and the ego-personality consciousness into taking action for the sole purpose of soul growth.

Most religions, and those of no affiliations with religions, believe evolution has never played a role in shaping the wisdom gained from our many lifetime experiences. And according to creationists, those who believe that God created everything also believe that mankind was created fully formed with having no previous related life or biology that belonged to other species of the past, like the ape, an insect, or a dinosaur, for example.

Religions and creationists believe that some parts of nature are too complex and confusing to be explained away by evolution. Therefore, they must be the handiwork of an intelligent designer, like God. Of course, these organizations may be overlooked because evolution could be God's tool for soul growth. If this was not so, how else could we get to know who we are, learn about the wisdom we possess and the choices we make?

In truth, we are the unspecified and nameless intelligent designers that have chosen to evolve through the process of evolution, and not that we are a product of some white male God that hates and loves at the same time. We are the Goddess and the product of having a series of learning experiences designed to repeat ourselves using a physical body as a prototype until we get to know ourselves as to all that is, for we are Christ and a living God-Goddess. Therefore, religions and creationists are somewhat correct as far as there is an "intelligent designer," but they fail to recognize the "intelligent designer" as the self.

It was you that formulated and created a "divine plan" to know "all that there is to know about consciousness and energy." And, reincarnation is used for fulfilling that "divine plan." And since we are infinite, we all have this deep desire to learn "all that there is to know about life and ourselves." And to do this, it is about our soul learning how to intermix with physical matter to emphasize the soul's divine sovereignty through the mental nature of soul growth, experiencing with ourselves through the ego, and experiencing with others while in the flesh.

In other words, our soul has gone through many versions of itself in developing our brain-mind, spirit, and physical body. Even to the point where we finally emphasized brains over brawns, which then gave us the language, creativity, reason, curiosity, and the most complex system that we can ever imagine, including the illusion of power, because energy is always neutral until activated by consciousness. This means one can activate that consciousness as to doing good, evil, or having compassion for other's choices.

Because of how we developed our mind-soul and consciousness journeying through time and space, lifetime after lifetime, we took on the belief that "like attracts like" or thoughts of "good and evil" attract thoughts of "good and evil," which was then taught to us by our family and religions.

Therefore, what we reflect or assign to money, power, our family, and our truths, we then attract to us the energy to what we assigned as power, family, truths, and how much of an issue money has over us.

This is also the same for our governments, the media, religion, friends, and businesses using power and money to control our truths, thereby controlling how we think and create our reality. It is not that money has power and is the root of all evil. We give our money away through our truths just as we give away our power to others by believing in the truth of others. And like power, money changes our thoughts about "who we truly are" and gives it to those that say we must fear God, and therefore be willing to spread that wealth to others by giving it to them.

Therefore, we place fear of power and money as becoming an issue in life, which then causes us to lose sight of our sovereignty as a Christ, God, and a Goddess. When religions teach that money is the root of all evil, they teach us to attract fear to ourselves not to have money. This even applies to the virus going around. Hence, it is not so much that we lack or fear money or the virus, it is that we lack the understanding of our truths connected to money, power, and the virus, and therefore, we believe it all to be conditional.

So, how can we attract money and health and alleviate power and our suffering if our truths are conditional? Stay true to yourself as being the creator of your world. Because of your consciousness path of evolution from the beginning stages of your awareness of existence, to where you have incarnated from insects to dinosaurs to mammals, and then to primates, has left a deep-rooted mark on what is "truth" when it comes to "who you truly are at your core."

For example, we gave up our freedom, power, individuality, and the truth of being Christ, God, and Goddess in our own right a long time ago to support an instilled intellectual truth for the benefit of feeling secure and being part of something. And all of it was instituted by religion, our intellect, and our politicians promising us that they will guide and protect us from ourselves as if they know better than we do.

It is incredible how we took on a false truth long ago about a white masculine-minded mental God that created us all because of taking on an attitude that everything is just too complex to understand when it comes to God, creation, and evolution. And now, we cannot get out of this false truth because of its hypnotic effects brought about by those in power. All of this is so overwhelming and powerful that we, by not realizing it, fell prey to a virus, a mask, and a vaccine that loves power and control, all because we were, and still are, unwilling to take full responsibility for our own acts of consciousness.

And the reason why those in power are so successful in keeping us in this hypnotic sleep state is that they tap into our pre-adolescent minds in much the same way they buy our votes with free programs and giveaways that keep us relying on them for our well-being. And the more they buy our loyalty, the more we become slaves to a socialist outcome that eventually turns to collectivism. That is when individual thought and creativeness die.

My friends, what is forgotten, the true nature of what religions call God-Goddess, is that we are absolute, divine, compassionate, unchangeable, unconditional and that we are in the form of Spirit Consciousness first and foremost. Thus, we are meant to be free agents and not that others should control us or our thoughts; otherwise, we become part of a robotic zombie culture consciousness.

Religions teach, without understanding its implications, by using the masculine Adam side of the mind as God instead of bringing the masculine and feminine together as one, like God-Goddess, we automatically fall into a consciousness of control and slavery. Why? Because everything is being created using a false God made of dual-energy; whereas, in the absoluteness of what we call energy, it only comes in as neutral until we, as a human, manipulate it according to our beliefs. And since this virus is made of three-dimensional dual-energy, so is the vaccine and those accepting it.

According to channeled information by Jesus and the ascended masters, God is not a person or a deity that carries any power over us. God is a "universal omnipresent mind field of pure unbiased, neutral energy" that reflects as "light" and is "absolute" and "unconditional." And as a Christ, we use this pure energy to create what we desire to manifest and experience. Hence, because of a desire to learn wisdom, we all decided on creating dual-energy that comes in many different frequencies, and therefore many different dimensions, truths, and experiences.

And now, after many incarnations, it is time to bring this dual-energy (false God) back to its original form as one, like husband and wife, and become balanced in all ways, including our own masculine and feminine nature. Thus, the remnants of what religion describes as God is nothing more than the masculine side of the mind in its intellectual state believing in power and taking control of all aspects of our Oversoul to keep the feminine, our spirit, squashed because the masculine feels our Oversoul (feminine) as a force that is of dark energy.

The unawakened masculine will always blame our Oversoul, the feminine, the divine side of self, for keeping sin alive and well, which then keeps our mind locked into a sleep state where we live, die, and suffer according to our truths. As in the opposite of our dualistic truths, this also means that God's true composition, which is very important to understand, is that we are Christ, God, and a Goddess having a consciousness that has the same composition as the Spirit of One. Therefore, we are infinite, unconditional, absolute, and divine.

And if we are these things, then we, as a Christ also, transformed this "universal omnipresent mind field of pure unbiased, neutral energy of light" into a molded energy composition that we happen to call God to use for our creations. Be it a star, a planet, a universe, an animal, a physical body, the air we breathe, and even a car, a table, for all things manifested, physical and non-physical, come from us as the creators transforming this "God energy of light" into a variety of dimensions, truths, beliefs, and manifestations to experience.

Again, the God that is understood as a white male supreme being who created us and all things is not an individual personality unto himself. The true God is the makeup of all Goddesses; you, me, and all humans alike. Therefore, we are spirit first and foremost, having a consciousness that is infinite, absolute, unchangeable, and divine. Otherwise, there would be no you, me, life, or earth.

Since God's inception long ago, religions have described God in a dualistic and physiological manner, existing only in the rational mind and ego, without having any physical evidence that God is an actual person that created all things, including our souls. Of course, Christian believers have proclaimed Jesus as the physical evidence of God in the flesh, and yet, Jesus has always expressed himself as pre-existing those with whom he spoke while he was on earth.

John, the apostle, who walked with Jesus, wrote that Jesus was with God in the very beginning, even before earth and man (John 1:1-5). In John 17-5, *"and now, father, glorify me in your presence with the glory I had with you before the world began."* And, of course, we cannot overlook John 10:30, where Jesus mentioned that *"he and the father are one."* And, if this is true, where do you think man, earth, the fish of the sea, the birds of the air, the animals, trees, water, the air we breathe, and what we all see as stars, planets, galaxies, and universe come from?

Again, my friends, what constituents the "composition" of these things is energy and that of the Christ within oneself, and not that these things are animated by some magical force or power that only comes from Jesus or some God outside of us. Therefore, if Jesus represents Christ as being part of our consciousness, where the expression of creation or the divine spark originated, then our own Christ consciousness would have to be the pause between the desire to create and the beginning itself.

Hence, if creation exists, then this "universal omnipresent mind field of pure unbiased, neutral energy of light (God)" has to be the explosion, and the Christ within us has to be the implosion, the movement, and the motivating spark because it takes consciousness, awareness, imagination, expression, compassion, and focus, notwithstanding sacred geometry, to bring everything into existence, including our human personality, mankind as a whole, even Jesus, and the Kingdom of One.

Therefore, since we are all in the image of this pure energy of light (God), then the in-breath of our Christ consciousness is the divine mother and the womb of all our creations awaiting the awareness of our consciousness to trigger the God masculine side of a dual-energy in manifesting our choices to experience. And since we are in the direct image of the Spirit of One, the Christ or Goddess, as we are her consciousness, then our choices must consist of having compassion, unity, focus (power), and that our expressions and creations must consist of this same universal pure God energy of light. This then causes the out-breath of form to appear, like earth or the physical body.

Hence, it is the Spirit of One (the Christ within us) that maintains the link between all souled beings as an extension of Christ, and not that we are some children of God as described by religion. Therefore, the out-breath of God (known as this universal energy of light) occurs simultaneously with the Christ (Goddess's) in-breath of our consciousness and with having no beginning and no end. Thus, we are the creator! Our Christ consciousness's in-breath becomes the final and absolute return of the form (physical) and formless (non-physical) back to the out-breath of our connection to this pure God energy of light for manifestation.

This means with the awakening of the Spirit of One, the mother-father God-Goddess within all souled beings, we eternally and simultaneously expressed and created into existence our Christ consciousness with equal authority and divineness. Hence, no soul is older, younger, has more power, or is better than another soul no matter if one is in spirit, in human form, or an extraterrestrial, black, white, yellow, brown, red, male, or female, brown-eyed or blue-eyed.

We Goddesses asked a long time ago to know God's truth and without having mystery tied to it. So, our Oversoul, our higher consciousness of spirit, committed itself to bring about the potential for us to learn this while still in human form. This is why we have many lifetimes to evolve into this understanding. Therefore, behind all things manifested, with or without form or matter, is our own Christ spirit (consciousness), giving it birth and life at some level.

Remember, truth is multi-dimensional like we are, for in its truest state, truth is unconditional and expansional, and it has always been because truth lets you be who you are and express who you are without being looked at as someone that is out of touch when it comes to the norm. In effect, truth is the wisdom of one's experiences coming through one's Christ consciousness, expressing itself through the human ego-personality. Therefore, there is no one truth! Your wisdom is the result of condensing all of your choices and experiences since your awakening in the first creation, then squeezing out the best of all lifetimes where your focus moves away from your dramas, lies, and heightened emotions; thus, in the end, your truths become your enlightenment, your wisdom, your realization, and your freedom.

As to Jesus and the Ascended Masters, it was you who created your soul, not some God outside of you. Your soul became part of your divine plan to fragment your Christ consciousness into multiple lifetime ego-personality aspects (clones) to learn about health, wealth, illness, poverty, lack of common sense, death, and many other things, including getting lost within your own consciousness. And this is why your Christ consciousness (Oversoul) is the holder of all your dark and light creations.

By the creation of your mental soul (Eve Principle), it gave you a chance to pretend that you didn't know who you truly are and where you came from for a while. Hence, your mental soul gave you the means to enter many physical bodies so you can evolve in wisdom and enlightenment to where you awaken in the physical as being a Christ in your own right. Once you, from the human ego, become enlightened to your Oversoul's divine plan, your stubborn ego-consciousness must ascend to where you can tap into the wisdom of your Oversoul's plan, which is what I am doing now. And it takes many lifetime experiences being lost and alone before you reach that frequency consciousness to connect with your Oversoul.

Thus, compassion is the divine sensitivity that gives you the wisdom of knowing that you are part of the Spirit of One's consciousness, which makes you part of the Christ consciousness equally as much as Jesus. And, as all souled beings, this means you are one with this Omnipresent Universal Divine Mind of Energy of Light, and all that is material, including the earth and everything in it. And yes, even those that do evil! Therefore, it becomes very important for everyone to understand the true meaning of the word "compassion" because it allows us to see the Spirit of One's consciousness and this God Energy of Light in a whole new way.

Why? Because from the beginning, our Christ spirit was patterned (and still is) in a divine unrestricted love state where it holds no form (physical body), no positive, no negative, no light, no dark, no guilt, no judgment, no sin, no fear, and no name, other than "I AM That I AM." However, once we were introduced to an emotional, mental mind and the perception of having a split consciousness that consists of two parts (outer and inner mental version), we took on an ego-Cain type of personality consciousness of forgetfulness and separation. This consciousness and energy then developed into positive and negative, which the Bible calls "the tree of knowledge of good and evil."

This means, when we first played in our divine state of non-dual energy and before our split consciousness, there was no avenue for us to express good and evil until we split our consciousness into two parts. Thus, giving us the means to move beyond our state of absolute divineness, oneness, and in accord with the Spirit of One and that of pure neutral Crystalline Energy. And since we are in the same harmonious essence as the Spirit of One and this universal mind field of pure Crystalline energy, there is no need for us to seek heaven because heaven is already part of our consciousness.

Chapter 14

EXPLORING HEAVEN AND HELL

Most of us on earth are not aware of our beginning, let alone who we truly are at our core and how we got to live upon the earth. Of course, the answers to these questions are found within our consciousness, to whom that is all that we are other than spirit. It is incredible how we do not understand that everything comes from spirit and consciousness. Even the energy that we use to create our experiences, good and bad, comes from consciousness. We have forgotten that our spirit's passion is to create and experience life in many different forms and ways and that passion always responds to consciousness.

Whether we are aware of our consciousness (spirit) as being the life-giver to the creations of our reality or not, just know that energy always responds to our consciousness acts. Thus, reality is born. Therefore, what I write here in this chapter may be for those who are ready to open up to the hidden secrets behind consciousness, and therefore, the meaning behind heaven and hell.

However, before we begin, we have to understand and appreciate, by the manifesting of our split mind and ego personalities of many, that our Christ consciousness can now learn what it is like to feel, expand, and get to know all things, rather than just be in a state of incompleteness. What do I mean by this?

When we, the Christ that we are, became aware of our consciousness eons ago about giving life to our creations and experiences, that is when we became aware of our existence. And if "I Exist as a Spirit," then "I AM" only of consciousness, the actual image of the Goddess. By being aware that "I Exist" in consciousness, then my spirit, because of its passion for learning its existence, created pure universal neutral energy (God) to experience itself in all possible ways. And that is when my spirit used its passion for expansion and soul growth.

And since we all are a Christ also, we went further with this expansion and desired to experience power, limitations, and everything in-between, like good and evil. Thus, our Christ consciousness, the feminine-Oversoul, using universal mind field of pure neutralized energy, created what is known today as our mind-soul and an ego-personality. This "act in consciousness" alone created a feeling as if our spirit, mind-soul, and ego were three instead of one. And, at the same time, they felt real and separate.

Because of having the awareness that our consciousness, and what gives life to whatever is imagined or conceived by our mind-soul, then at the beginning of our creating activity eons ago, everything about ourselves was then based on consciousness without having any wisdom or understanding of making choices. Thus, this created a feeling within us of not knowing who we were. That is when we spirits developed a passion for moving forward in consciousness to learn and understand the questions about "who we were" and what is our mind-soul and ego-personality all about.

And that is why, in our beginning stages of awareness, we all were of no form because "all that there was in the beginning" was only consciousness. And because of our spirit not knowing what consciousness was all about in our beginning stages of imaging and creating, we felt a kind of fear growing within our consciousness that we didn't understand. So, to understand that fear, we spirits then chose to say farewell to our Christ consciousness, the Goddess within, and went on to explore the questions, "Who am I and why am I only of consciousness?" And "Why do I have a mind-soul and ego that are not defined so I can understand myself?"

These questions and more led us down a path of feeling nervous. It was a nervousness that was never experienced before. And due to this nervousness, we spirits began to feel uneasy about the choice we made to separate our masculine mental and ego consciousness from our Christ consciousness. Thus, causing uneasiness, uncertainty, doubt, and the fear of losing our awareness of being a "consciousness of neutrality and oneness."

This "act in consciousness" led us to separate ourselves from our own Christ consciousness (Oversoul), where we entered into a consciousness of a masculine-feminine mental soul consciousness that created an energy that became opposing to each other called dual-energy. And with this opposing energy, it carried a "vibrational frequency" that vibrated as up and down, good and bad, right and wrong, positive and negative. And that is when we took on a strong belief that this energy appeared as light and dark. Thus, leaving us very confused!

This confusion led to chaos because we found this "opposing energy" ripping our "oneness of a Christ consciousness" into billions and billions of pieces of itself that ended up being a great number of potentials and lifetimes for us to experience. Of course, this does not mean we have billions and billions of lifetimes, even though we could. It is just that we ended up creating billions and billions of potentials for us to experience good (light), evil (dark), and neutrality.

However, once we entered into this "energy of two" (positive and negative), we then began to rebel against our Christ consciousness by believing that the perfection we once held as a balanced masculine-feminine god-goddess consciousness is no longer part of our consciousness or spirit. Thus, setting ourselves up to rebel against our own Christ consciousness. Not only did we do that, but we also began to rebel against each other.

This caused us to fall in consciousness to a lower energy frequency where we believed the masculine, or positive side of the mind, was indeed the powerhouse behind the throne, while our feminine soul side became the consciousness of responsibility. And this is where we structured our ego-consciousness into a clone personality that made us feel separated, free, and powerful. This belief in power caused us to explore a consciousness of light and dark, known as "the tree of knowledge of good and evil" in Genesis, Chapter Two. And this consciousness movement ended up becoming our biggest challenge when it came to bringing our masculine-positive and our feminine-negative consciousness back into balance or back to its neutrality state again.

It was a time when we souls entered into a belief so strong that we saw our consciousness, two-fold; having an outer consciousness and an inner subconsciousness that eventually gave birth to an ego-personality clone that strongly believed in power. And because of this strong belief in power, we completely became unaware that we cannot create life, positive or negative, without the help of our Christ consciousness participating. And this includes our thoughts, truths, and the energy we use for our creations, even the use of our mind and ego.

Therefore, without the basic understanding of our Christ consciousness and the energy we use at our core being neutral in all that we create to experience, religion will always misunderstand our consciousness role, no matter at what dimensional frequency we operate from. Without this understanding, we become very mental, logical, and scholarly when it comes to knowing God-Goddess, Heaven, and Hell.

As mentioned, our Christ consciousness is all that we are at our core, leaving everything else just an illusion. And by religion misunderstanding consciousness, they overlook the truth about heaven and hell as being a place where we go after death, but is, in fact, a place in consciousness that we can choose to experience at any time. Therefore, to understand heaven and hell, we need to be aware that our Christ consciousness is the creator of our experiences, good and evil.

Know that Heaven and Hell are a choice to experience and not as a place we go after death. This misinterpretation of Heaven and Hell by religion has been going on since religion's inception. And since the masculine side of the mind controls every creative act because of one's ego-personality's belief in power, then it is all up to you, and not some God above or church that determines your fate when it comes to Heaven and Hell.

For example, like religion, when the system says God knows best for us, they are really saying the masculine side of our mind and ego knows best. So, think about that! It means that religion, and all those in power, knows what is best for you and not you, which is why they, along with governments, are so desperate to keep you asleep to the truth. If we learned to quiet our minds and listen to our intuitive consciousness instead of our emotions before making choices, our Oversoul (Christ) would come in and guide us.

What happened is that we became spiritual hobbyists engaged in a belief that heaven and hell are somehow outside of us as a place we go after death, instead of becoming a conscious creator of what we really desire to experience as our reality. How many times do we pray for protection from the devil and for God to give us enlightenment, abundance, and healing? And yet, nothing happens! It does not happen because we keep focusing on "not being conscious" of our "consciousness" being the Christ and the source of those things. Instead, we are so focused on the masculine side of our mental mind and ego-personality without considering the Christ part of us that is the Goddess we should be paying attention to. After all, our Christ consciousness is the source that gives our mind and the clone ego the authority to manifest our desires to experience.

My friends, religion, and society are programmed into believing that the masculine side of the mind and one's ego-personality is the source and authoritative power in all of creation, leaving out one's Christ spirit (Oversoul-Goddess), having no say or power. This is why religion, and that of society, places all authority on a masculine God that holds to itself the belief in good and evil, right and wrong, heaven and hell, as being the creator of "all that is," which of course, is false. Therefore, know that the God of the Bible is a false God because the real God-Goddess is always about life as being absolute and a consciousness that is unchangeable.

Hence, to discover "Heaven and Hell," the real God and Goddess, and who we are at our core essence, we need to discover our own Christ consciousness and our divine story as being a God, Goddess, and a Christ in our own right first. Know when we spirits became aware of our Christ consciousness for the first time, we became aware that we are the extensions of the Spirit of One because we are her consciousness, and not that we are some children of a God that shows itself as dual-energy. We are her consciousness, equal to and not less than a Christ in our own right.

Because her consciousness is our consciousness, having no beginning or end, then only what is Absolute Consciousness and Energy is life and not what one considers death. However, once our consciousness gave life to a universal mind field of a masculine unlimited energy of pure and neutral light, it allowed our Christ consciousness to split from a consciousness of one to a consciousness of two. This allowed us to see ourselves, like in a mirror, as one side of us took on the role of a masculine mind (Adam), while the other side of us took on an emotional, mental soul consciousness of record where it (Eve) recorded everything that the masculine mind side chose to experience.

This is where in Genesis, the Goddess (our Christ consciousness) asked Adam (the masculine, the positive side of our mind), and Eve (the feminine, the negative side of that same mind), and one's soul record of responsibility about being naked. Being "naked" actually means when we first exposed ourselves to a dualistic consciousness that produced opposing energy to play with that was the beginning of the fall in consciousness.

And when our Christ consciousness (Goddess) cast out Adam, Eve, and the Serpent from higher consciousness (Garden), it characterizes our neutralized consciousness of a higher frequency becoming part of a three-dimensional consciousness, as our spirit, mind-soul, and ego clone-personality became the trinity for the "Father, Son, and Holy Spirit. Therefore, to whom we call the Children of God are those many ego-personality clones or aspects of the self that are spread throughout many dimensions.

When our Christ consciousness passed down all authority to our mind of the masculine (the Son) and its partner, the soul consciousness of responsibility, that is when our mind-soul of the masculine and feminine took control of the creating process. And in the process, we created an ego-personality of persuasion as this is represented by the Serpent and that of Cain, convincing our mental mind-soul to follow an emotional agenda to lose ourselves in our own creations. Then, as we all know, according to the story of Adam, Eve, and the Serpent, our ego-personality of persuasion took complete control of our energy in manifesting our truths, desires, and choices here on earth.

It was the only way for our Christ consciousness to remain pure, unchangeable, and absolutely free from using dual-energy. When we look at God's essence as only masculine and having a mind that only deals with opposites or duality, we overlook the most important part of God. And, that is, the feminine side (the Goddess) because that is the real side of us that only gives life and not the masculine or ego side of self. When we fail to see our spirit's feminine Christ side of self (male or female) as life itself, we overlook our own divinity.

Without our spirit or Christ consciousness, the masculine mental mind side of self and our defiant ego-personality become nothing. Why? Because they have no power. It is all an illusion created by the belief in it coming from working out of the mind and ego! This means, without our Christ consciousness, there would be no use for pure universal neutral energy (God) because there would be no you, no me, no universe, and no mental soul consciousness for us to gain wisdom. In other words, how can we, on a mental level, have an out-breath if we don't have an in-breath first (spirit-Christ consciousness)?

What gives our masculine, positive side of the mind and our ego-personality of persuasion life is the infinite in-breath of our own Christ spirit, also known as the feminine Oversoul consciousness. Therefore, our spirit (the Christ) is the only part of us that is real! And since our posturing and persuasive ego-personality comes from the masculine mental and rational side of a deceptive mind, and not from our Christ consciousness, even though it animated it with life, it will always come between our mental soul side (Eve), our Christ spirit (Oversoul), and our outer masculine side (Adam) in keeping us asleep to the real Christ, you.

This is how Jesus became a Christ in his own right. He awakened to the truth of being God, Goddess, Christ, and a creative ego version (clone) of himself in the flesh. This is what we have to do also, become awakened to this procedure. In other words, he brought all parts and pieces of his fragmented consciousness, his energy, and became one body of consciousness again while in the flesh.

It is not that we only work with spirit or Christ consciousness. It is that we have to learn to balance our masculine side of the mind, our mental soul side, and all our ego-personality aspects working as one consciousness. You know, God is one, as you are God, Christ, the Goddess, and a clone ego version in the flesh becoming awakened as a sovereign divine being in your own right. Remember, "consciousness" is all that we are, and it cannot be taken over unless we allow our masculine side of the mind and ego-personality to control all that we express in consciousness.

So, if we believe strongly in heaven and hell, good and bad, right and wrong, light and dark, and have fear, then those beliefs need to be answered in the form of us experiencing them in the flesh. It is that simple! If you do not want to experience any more karma, then let go of the belief in a punishing God. How can God be a punishing God if there is no such thing as sin or dual-energy (positive and negative) because everything is derived from neutral energy? It is just when this neutral energy reaches the mind of the masculine within; it chooses according to what it believes as truth and what it chooses to use as energy.

This is seen and felt as our truths because our mind and ego-personality operate based on false truths, even though we may see ourselves creating good experiences. Nevertheless, in the end, the mind and ego will always find a way to destroy what we consider good experiences. Know that the difference between our "consciousness," our "mind," and our "ego" needing to be understood is that we will always find ourselves giving animation and application to what we believe is true for us, like having a physical body, to play out those applications.

Also, know that our mind and our ego are what gives life and application to our emotions and not our Christ consciousness and to whom is the real you! Your Christ consciousness only acts on passion and intuitive feelings without any definition other than "I Exist." Hence, your Christ consciousness becomes an observer for your mind and ego behaviors in gaining wisdom from the experiences chosen. Therefore, it is not about sin, right, or wrong. It is about your experiences and the wisdom gained from them. Know that enlightenment is not about how much we know or understand about

God from an intellectual or ego level. It is about becoming conscious and aware of how our masculine and feminine consciousness, along with our ego, are out of balance.

Of course, it is not about blaming a man or woman either, because it is about the masculine, the feminine, and the ego within the self working against each other. Know that karma is a choice because we are not our past lifetimes, and we are not our sins either. It is all about stealing energy and believing that we have to be good to make it to heaven.

It is not about being evil or wrong either when it comes to karma. It is about our religious training over centuries in believing in a God that is good and a devil that is evil, keeping us cycling through many karmic incarnations. It comes down to the realization of who we truly are and who we are not. I hope this brought some clarity to you.

Chapter 15

STEALING ENERGY

I would like to clarify something from the Bible where it is mentioned in Revelation 7:3-8, 7:4, 14:1, and 14:3-5 about the significance of the 144,000 tribes of Israel. This number does not mean what you think it means, as the number refers to the 144,000 different soul families, no more and no less. Thus, the "sealing of the 144,000" found in Revelation 7:4 is symbolic in describing the number of the many different angelic soul groups that have left higher consciousness long ago and has nothing to do with Jews.

In fact, according to Jesus and the Ascended Masters, the word "Jews" itself is referring to all of us souls that left higher consciousness eons ago to explore a three-dimensional world called Earth. Paul in 2 Corinthians 1:22 explains that God has *"set his seal of ownership on us,"* which means us souled beings here on earth, with no exceptions, are part of what is called the Jews. And by religion overlooking the meaning of the word "Israel" and why it was used for us souled beings here on earth as being the makeup of the 144,000 soul families, it caused us to believe that the Jews are the chosen people of God.

Perhaps you have read the story of how Jacob's name was changed to Israel after he had wrestled with a "man" all night. And because of his success, Jacob obtained a blessing from God (Genesis 32:25-33), where he became known as the Prince of God. And since all mankind is noted in Genesis as being a Child of God, even though we are God, then you, me, and all souls are part of the 144,000 spoken about in the Book of Revelation.

As Jacob struggles were to get back to his birthplace, then it is the same for all of us souled beings, as we too are struggling to find our way back to our birthplace, back to higher consciousness. Of course, this birthplace is not our human birthplace but is about the birthplace of our "awareness of being a Christ also." It is about becoming aware of our Christ consciousness as to whom we indeed are in the scheme of things.

Within these 144,000 thousand soul families, a few of us, including a dark-minded soul family, felt that we humans here on earth needed some guidance in our lives. So, after many years of living in the physical under peace and harmony, this particular dark-minded soul family fell to a Cain consciousness of greed, power, and control. And then, they believed exclusively that they were better than any other soul family. Thus, they took that power and began to rule over us and the earth as if they own it.

Remember, when a few of us from each souled family decided to come to earth in the physical, we all, at first, worked from out of a mind (masculine-feminine) and ego-personality that was quite neutralized and balanced (represented by Adam, Eve, and the Serpent in the Garden before being kicked out by God). And this was because, at the beginning of our appearance here on earth in the physical, we all were Goddesses (Christ) that generated our own neutralized energy to use for our creations. It was much later that we souls began to appropriate the energy of two, which then is where we fell in consciousness.

In other words, since we were an extension of the Spirit of One, we souls, as a Christ unto ourselves, owned and possessed the same quality of pure neutralized energy as the Spirit of One because together, we are the Christ-spirit of One. This means no one is higher or lower than our Christ consciousness, and therefore we each own our energy. It was not that we souled beings (Goddesses) had to borrow energy or get it from someone else to survive. Each and every one of us Christ beings created this pure energy for self-use, and it belonged to each soul member, and therefore we never needed to borrow it or steal it from somewhere or someone.

However, since our Christ spirit passed down all authority to the masculine mind side of that same consciousness, including choice, we lost our awareness of being the creator and the source, the Goddess. It was up to our mind of the masculine within the self to keep this pure infinite energy flowing to keep our mind and ego-personality free from ever becoming limited with our creations. But, because of losing our awareness of being a Christ, we also believed energy came to us by some source outside of ourselves.

The example is shown in Genesis as Adam, Eve, and the Serpent (our ego) being kicked out of the Garden, as they were all part of the first creation at the beginning of our awakening as a Christ and a God. But later, because of the belief in separation, we forgot we were Christ. Remember, God is just symbolic of pure universal energy. But, as everyone knows, the Serpent (our cunning ego-personality) began to influence our mind and soul consciousness of record and responsibility into choosing to separate themselves from that part of us that makes us a Christ in our own right.

Therefore, once we souled beings came to earth in the physical, and after many lifetimes playing with this new energy of two (positive and negative), we began to adulterate this pure neutralized energy by judging it to be as light and dark, good and bad, right and wrong, opposite of neutralization. And that is what caused us to steal energy!

This was also the beginning of our Cain ego-personality consciousness, which had no power or authority of his own, through the misunderstanding of his purpose, he activated a cunning way to steal energy from our Christ consciousness and from the masculine side of the mind to stay alive, and in control, which was to kill our awareness of being Christ in the flesh, and is symbolized by the killing of Abel. And that is when the thought bubbled up from within our cunning ego-Cain personality to steal energy that allowed our ego to feel that it had power. Thus, creating a belief in control.

Our ego's cunningness (the Cain Principle) deceived and fooled us at the time in believing the best way to control power and own it was to have our masculine side of the mind perceive that it was a creation from someone higher, more powerful, and mightier than itself. Hence, the ego-personality then manipulated our mind, since our ego has no authority or power of its own, and found the avenue to become very powerful, controlling, and demanding. Thus, making itself a god and the ruler of choices, when in fact, all that our Cain ego did was persuade the masculine side of the mind to believe in power.

This eventually led to the creation of a God of morality, a God of logic, a God of worship, and a God of sin, death, and punishment, and yet, all of it is not real. Therefore, in the symbolization of this takeover by the cunningness of our Cain ego-personality, the Bible used the "Belialians" as to recognizing the soul family that decided to steal our energy and cloud our mind into believing that we were all created by a God that has the same characteristics and prevailing tendencies to act in a manner as being our God. And yet, this God, acting as our creator, is actually masquerading around as both the Devil and God. And who is this soul family that worships this Cain consciousness? It was, and still is, the Reptilian race.

People overlook the idea of there being more than just Earth where humans play. There are many planets and multidimensional realms where souls hang out. Remember, everything is life, and no such thing as death when it comes to the real God. By realizing that our "belief systems" are the keys to keeping us asleep, this Reptilian soul family seized all structured communities worldwide, including the creating of religion and who we need to worship as a God. And this family accomplished it by incarnating here on earth as our leaders and scholars since the beginning of earth millions of years ago.

At first, we humans were free from them because of being aware of whom we were, but as time moved forward, incarnation after incarnation, the first thing the Reptilian family did, along with other negative families, was sculpture themselves as gods and then rewrite scripture in order to present to us a God of fear, a God of conditional love, hate, judgment, sin, death, and punishment, and a god to worship to control our minds and beliefs. These dark-minded soul families knew that they could only survive if they stole our energy. Thus, they targeted the first church that was introduced to the world. And from there, they focused on acquiring all society's leadership positions.

Just look at Jesus when he walked the earth over two thousand years ago and how he was put to death by religion and those governments in power, all because he taught unconditional love, reincarnation, no judgment, no sin, and no punishment. However, at the same time, Jesus tried to make clear of creating one's own karma. Even the subject of reincarnation was looked at by religious authorities as something ridiculous. Therefore, the religion's remedy was to shut Jesus up by putting him to death for blasphemy and then have the people follow him as God and our savior a few hundred years after his death. Jesus' death gave them the avenue to create a religious belief in having us needing a savior.

This example shows how this dark-minded Reptilian family steals our energy to keep their power and control over us and the world. It is this same soul family that has introduced us to the mask wearing and the vaccine. You see, this dark-minded soul family, because of working from the Cain consciousness, presumed that power and the source of life come from energy and not from consciousness. Thus, they adopted a strong belief that they must steal our energy (blood), not only to control us but to survive. Also, with them not realizing they were controlling our consciousness to maintain their power as well. They logically, intellectually, and from a Cain consciousness, viewed themselves as superior beings to the human race.

Therefore, they created a hierarchy system and then placed themselves at the top. Today, their control is finally slipping away because Earth's energy is rising in frequency to a fifth-dimensional frequency, which causes us, humans, to awaken. However, to hide their identity here on earth, they must work hard to keep us asleep and unaware of their dark intentions; otherwise, this energy and consciousness frequency will eliminate them from the earth and place them on another planet that is still dealing with three-dimensional energy.

The struggles we go through here on earth every day to gain our freedom against this hierarchy system continue today by us humans following economic suppression, political coverups, and mental programming by our politicians, even our religious teachers are preaching to us about us needing a savior outside of us. And to top it off, they feed us a belief in a false god that we must worship and fear or else. For example, look how they used a virus, the mask, and their vaccine to keep us in fear and under their control.

This Reptilian soul family has become very much disconnected and insensitive to other soul families that live here on earth. Thus, keeping us all in a framework of being a slave to their everyday needs for them to stay alive and in control. However, this dark-minded soul family is beginning to lose the battle in keeping us asleep because every day, this energy frequency of the earth is rising to a level that they cannot stand it much longer.

Look how we, the people of the United States, have lost our way with interpreting the Constitution and how our politicians ignore it for their benefit. And we, the people, allow it without even a thought about them stealing our energy and our creative consciousness to benefit them. Look how we all have become servants to them as if they are our Gods and we are their subjects. And these very dark-minded Reptilian souls place it right in our faces. And we ignore it because they play us against each other by branding us as a democrat, a republican, a Catholic, a Jew, an Arab, color versus color, gender versus gender, race versus race, and many other dualistic techniques. And what do we do? We allow them to brand us, not realizing we are of one family, the Christ consciousness family.

Throughout the Bible, we can find passages where this Reptilian God has caused us nothing but pain, contradictions, and many afflictions because we fail to wake up and take responsibility for our own creations. Moses' ten commandments were supposedly given as divine laws in order for us to follow and become more holy (Exodus 20:17). And yet, this Reptilian God of the Bible broke every commandment. Just look in Judges 7:22-23; God causes the Midianites to kill one another. In 1 Samuel 14:20-23, God confuses the Philistines and causes them to kill one another.

In 2 Kings 6:18, God inflicts a number of people with blindness because Elisha asks him to do so. And, in 2 Kings 8:1, God causes a famine without specifying a reason. Also, in Genesis 12:11-17, when Abraham sees the Egyptians approaching his camp, he tells his wife that they may kill him and rape her, so to avoid this, he told his wife, Sarah, to act like she is his sister. However, because of the lie, eventually, the Pharaoh had sexual encounters with Abraham's wife; thus, God sending plagues upon Pharaoh and his people as punishment for sleeping with another man's wife.

Why would a true loving God do that? Especially since Pharaoh did not know that she was married. As we can see, all of this is designed to steal energy from us to keep this Reptilian God of the Bible and their religions of humanity alive in order to keep our vibrations from rising. Thus, they continue today in maintaining their power and control over us by using religion and a God of dual-energy as something real.

This is why the Reptilian soul family seized the real God's identity a long time ago and replaced it with a deceptional and emotional God of duality, power, and control just to steal our energy and our consciousness to create what they wanted and not what we wanted to experience. Have you ever heard God speak to you like those of the church claim God speaks to them? Probably not! When this God speaks to them, the subject is always based on an emotional response to right and wrong, light and dark, good and evil, God and the Devil, money, and war. This is because everything from religion and the Bible is always based on sin, fear, duality, money, and war.

For example: Black versus white, republican versus democrats, religion versus religion, nation versus nation, people versus the IRS, all in the name of power, control, and keeping us asleep to steal our energy and money. We are essentially their power source, like a battery, for their creations. Actually, our creations are based on their belief systems and their free will to choose and not ours because we follow what they tell us to follow blindly without any question about why all because of believing in a God, a religion, and politicians that love power, money, and control.

Remember, the more a soul separates itself from its own Christ spirit, knowing that one has infinite energy around them all the time, the more the soul moves into the shadows of disconnecting itself even more from their Christ self and their infinite pure energy (the source). Thus, not only becoming a slave to the system but having to steal energy yourself to stay alive. We can see this with people all around us, along with our religion and governments, trying to steal our money, home, health, and who we truly are by continually feeding them our energy as if we are their food to keep them alive.

We do not realize that our consciousness and energy have become owned and controlled by all those that teach us what is right and wrong, good and evil, and that we need to worship God the same way we despise the Devil. Thus, we have become their slaves and food bank. Look at our political parties and see how much energy stealing is going on around them and us. See how they keep us in fear by telling us one party is better than the other. They also tell us how much we don't have, while others have plenty. Therefore, we need the government to keep it all balanced without realizing that our government is trying to place us all under a strict lockdown of ever knowing our creative power to be free and sovereign.

These Reptilian elites incarnated into human form are leaders of our religions and governments from all levels, and they take from us, who work hard, to give to those who are lazy and do not want to work, thereby giving them the energy needed to place us and those that are lazy under their control by using giveaways (or free stuff) to continue stealing our energy, therefore our lives. All of this energy stealing is about power, money, control, and keeping us disconnected from our own Christ consciousness, or otherwise, they would not be able to exist on this planet.

We all have been stuck in a deceptive mind and an ego prison that only understands power as real and that we need to get some to survive. My friends, power is an illusion, and it has been used by this dark-minded soul family for manipulation and control for a long time now. Also, do not be confused because Jesus and the Ascended Masters mentioned the Reptilian soul family. It is to understand that before coming to earth, we humans also belonged to a spiritual family just as we belong to a human family here on earth now. Remember, there are 144,000 different soul families, and many of them are very loving, compassionate, and kind.

We, family groups, incarnated into human form, as one's brother can be from the Reptilian family while one's sister can be from a different soul group family. However, know that most Reptilians do incarnate into the same family bloodline, as they like to keep the bloodline pure to maintain their power and control. They incarnate as big business owners, big banking elites, executives of large corporations, Royals, Hollywood elites, Media celebrities, politicians, big tech owners, and most Reptilians love to incarnate as our religious scholars and leaders of our churches.

As mentioned earlier in the book, we all have lost our free will to choose because we are too busy following others' free will because of not willing to open up our minds to what is happening all around us. We are so mentally programmed, like a virus, and the only way to keep this virus alive is to keep us in fear, as this and all diseases are man-made, and we swallowed it hook, line, and sinker all because of our religious and family beliefs and the trust in our politicians. And we humans are allowing it by not taking responsibility for our own awakening.

We fail to look at this God of the Bible and our religious leaders as implants that keep us stuck in a vibrational energy signature of duality that has placed our consciousness in a hypnotic sleep state that keeps us coming back to earth over and over again to be food (energy) for them. You see, not only do they want to control us while on earth in the flesh, but they also want to control us after our death.

Because of believing everything outside of us is real, including power and those of you who attend some religious church, thinking they will be saved, we will continue our suffering until we come to an awakening to the falseness of it all. Energy is always free to those awakened because they have realized that they are the ones that create their own energy. Everything they perceive as energy is built upon them, knowing they are its creator and no one else.

However, to those that refuse to awaken only see energy as something outside of themselves; thus, they become the victim of energy stealing, many incarnations, and karma. And we wonder why we are sick, have no money, and seem lost, as energy stealing can come in many forms. As someone mentioned, and I quote, "One is not just a small grain of sand on the beach. One is the whole beach!"

The human ego-personality is the part of you that experiences the flesh, while the Christ consciousness part of you receives the wisdom of the experiences. Thus, there never was a divine plan in reality, even though we call it a divine plan. It is just our natural state of being aware of the Christ consciousness within the self, while the mind and ego take on the responsibility to choose enlightenment.

Chapter 16

THE MYTH OF PUTTING OTHERS FIRST

Most of us are considerably stressed out these days, as people are more divided today than ever before, and it can be found worldwide. Why is that? According to the channeled materials received by Jesus and the Ascended Masters, it has to do with many things, but the top stress maker on the list is "putting others first before self." Believe it or not, the Ascended Masters have stated in many channelings that by serving others first before self, we overlook the basic spiritual healing formula recognized as "compassion," as it is one of the keys to one's awakening and healing. The others on the list are deep breathing, allowing, and not knowing the Rapture is in full bloom.

Of course, one would think because of all the polarity going on in the world today, especially with the United States people and their religion and politics, that "putting others first" would be at the bottom of the list. But, if one studies politics and religion, one would find that people want to be lied to because they are afraid of responsibility. People would rather have their politicians and their church lie to them because it takes away responsibility.

People do not want to hear the truth because truth usually carries the emotional baggage of accountability and the fear of past lifetimes even if one does not believe in past lifetimes. However, it is somehow felt deep within one's soul but very much ignored because of fear. People only want to hear stuff that will make them feel good and not make them feel uncomfortable. For example, people want religion to preach and tell them that their sins can be taken away if they just adhere to what the church tells them about what God wants them to do to get forgiveness and healing.

It comes down to people feeling secure and good about themselves by working hard to please others before themselves. Of course, when serving others first before self, according to Jesus and the ascended masters, religion and our politicians end up stealing our energy, power, and our divine right as a sovereign being without even realizing we are allowing them to create our reality to experience. How can we help others if we do not know how to take care of ourselves first on a spiritual level?

Nonetheless, to help understand what is being said, let's research the meaning of "compassion" by using the American Dictionary. According to the dictionary, the standard meaning refers to unity, harmony, and sympathy for others. Therefore, it is interpreted as helping others before self and how it sounds like the right and moral thing to do. And this is where religion and our politicians come in and make sure we follow the golden rule by having us feel emotional toward protecting our family, country, religion, and our political parties at all costs, even to death if necessary. And yet, all of it is based on a lie, fear, and the belief that our answers must come from outside of self.

But, from the angelic realm, "compassion" holds a whole new meaning because of free will and our authority to choose as a divine sovereign being. Therefore, it becomes extremely crucial to allow ourselves not to interfere with anyone's free will to choose what they desired to experience as their reality. Suppose one's desire is to experience cancer, joy, or being a person of immorality, or just being a gracious person. In that case, as a sovereign Christ being in their own right, we must allow them to experience what they choose without any interference coming from another sovereign Christ being, you or me, and that means praying to a God for them to heal.

It is okay to say a prayer as long as it is said in such a way that it does not interfere with their free will to choose and their sovereignty as a Christ to experience whatever they are asking God to help them heal. In other words, it is about "allowing" one to be a sovereign Christ in their own right, and therefore, the prayer should be focused on the will of the one that is ill and not on the one saying the prayer to heal them.

To understand compassion, we need to understand that "energy is more than just energy" and "consciousness is more than just consciousness." And since energy was born from consciousness, then energy, in its purest state, when operating at a divine quantum frequency, is neutral until charged by the polarity of a reality that is placed with one's mind and one's many ego personalities as something real. And since our consciousness is the core essence of us being a Christ also, and nothing less, it creates energy as it creates life experiences, all according to where one's energy signature is vibrating. Some call this "energy signature" one's DNA, which actually means the power and strength of the "Divine Natural Attribute" of the Christ consciousness.

Know that, for example, when we hear the priest give a prayer during a mass, saying, "For thy am the power and the glory, and the Kingdom now and forever," and then the congregation finishes up by saying, "Amen." What we are actually doing by saying "Amen" is giving away our power as a divine being, our glory as a Christ also, and our consciousness (kingdom) away to religion "now and forever." Thus, leaving us bound to a belief system where we are the source of energy for the church and for their existence, "now and forever."

In other words, we become stuck in a three-dimensional consciousness, "now and forever," or as long as we are asleep to the practice of the church and their energy stealing. What is not being presented to us by the world's religions is that we, as divine beings, already know everything there is to know about our divinity, our Christ consciousness, and the divine power of energy, which cannot be taught to us by anyone person anyway, including religion. Why? Because it is not about teaching us about these things. It is about helping us to remember who we are as a sovereign divine being in our own right.

What has been forgotten is that you are the King of your "dominion" (consciousness); otherwise, there would be no God, Goddess, nor would there be choices to learn wisdom. Therefore, "I Exist" as a sovereign God and Goddess unto myself and "I AM" the creator of my own experiences. And it is the same for all of us, good or evil. We create our own world with our "words" and with our "belief systems." Thus, it is not about praying for healing for someone else. It is about decreeing that you are the Christ and the savior of yourself. So, then heal yourself by declaring you are the Christ savor of you.

Therefore, choosing the forgoing conclusion if healing is what you desire, then decree it to be so on a conscious level. Remember, there is no such thing as sin! It is just you "acting in consciousness" by way of your own words, declaring your divine power (good or evil) to be employed and activated in manifesting those words for you to experience. Of course, all that is left when those words are manifested is for you to take full responsibility for them, which means no one else can do it for you, not even Jesus.

When we understand our consciousness as being the core essence of our creations and not in any intellectual or literal term, consciousness then is about being responsible for ourselves as a creator. Therefore, nothing can exist outside of our creations unless we first created it for us to experience, which is why we must have compassion for those that are experiencing what they are experiencing. Hence, what we hear, feel, taste, see, smell, touch, and believe as material living, including our suffering is not only an illusion or hologram. It is about you creating every bit of it!

We think and feel it as real because we are experiencing it from a mental, physical, and ego consciousness using a vibrational energy frequency that moves back and forth, up and down, good and bad, light and dark, right and wrong, positive and negative as the source. In other words, an energy of opposites, and yet it is all an illusion, which is why there is no such thing as death because God, as we understand God, is nothing but life. Therefore, it comes down to nullifying all the contracts that you had made with your divinity and with all your lifetimes past, and then declaring to yourself that you are an "I AM Christ" in your own right.

Then you can ascend like in a Rapture to the fifth dimension. Know from within your core essence as a Christ long ago, you chose the energy you desired to display outward, good or evil, and today you are displaying that energy from what you chose. Therefore, the choice is your responsibility. And if you chose Earth Energy and a physical body to experience karma, then that choice belongs to you and not to the one that wants you to heal or stay around longer. By not being aware of this underlying spiritual truth, it can cause you to surrender to a devilish energy of such denseness that you actually forfeit having any healing, becoming abundant, and experiencing many joys in life.

You can see this worldwide, as people live in poverty, have endless health problems, and the joys of life are so few. All because of the misunderstanding of compassion and who God and Christ are at the quantum level! Not only did we do that, but how we also misunderstood consciousness, the process of allowing, having free will, and the misjudging of energy at its core attribute as being divine and neutral (natural). Through our own DNA (divine natural attribute), we confirm what energy we will choose in manifesting our beliefs and experiences in any given lifetime. So be careful of your thoughts, your words, and how you choose what you want to put behind those words and thoughts because it could mean a lifetime of suffering.

When we first moved our focus outside of our own "oneness of a higher consciousness" eons ago, we fell under a hypnotic belief that dual-energy, positive and negative, was real, when in fact, this dual-energy was put in place by us spirits choosing it to experience our choices to learn wisdom, and this includes responsibility. However, because of the influences of these two controlling energies brought about by our strong belief in it, we, as sovereign spiritual beings, fell into the trap of discovering many diverse stories (lifetimes) and commentaries where we took on many roles that corresponded to various views of truths (lies) that caused us to take on karma (the sowing and reaping) found in the Bible.

My friends, we have been lied to for centuries about serving others first before ourselves, and it has been at a significant cost to our health, our safety, our karma, and our happiness. Instead, we see a world in chaos, and therefore, we need someone like Jesus to come along and save us from ourselves. This, my friends, is all coming from the dark forces, having us believe we need a savior. Come to know that most of what we have heard and have seen are just about the opposite of what we have been told and have seen.

We have been trapped in a mind that works on our emotional ties to a God of polarity that only values serving others as the key to reaching heaven and understanding. And all of it is tied to stealing our soul, our energy, and our consciousness in what it produces to create their reality and not our own. When we learn to have complete compassion for ourselves, first and then others, that is when we can do more for others than just pray for them and give them money.

When Jesus walked the earth, he became Christ in the flesh, and that is when he realized that serving himself first allowed him to serve others on a much larger and deeper scale than just feeding and healing them. It is the same with our governments and how they keep on passing laws to help the poor. And all that they are doing is hurting the poor! It seems as if we are running around acting like we are a seeker of light when, in reality, we seek more darkness and lies just to feel comfortable and safe by saying, "Look how much I give to others." Thus, we end up having more lifetimes suffering the consequences of our righteous teachings about serving others first.

We serve others by our words and belief in sin as being real, that God is judgmental and punishable, that God is angry, our talk about death, and how we could spend life in eternal hell or some majestic heaven if we just make sure others come first before self. All of this comes from dualistic Earth Energy and not from our Christ consciousness. When the choice was made eons ago by our outer masculine side of the mind to experience every aspect of life, good and evil, our feminine soul side gave that choice, life. And this is what moved us into an ego-personality consciousness of balance that eventually birthed us into the physical world of creating unbalanced energy to work out in an opposing way.

Can you imagine your excitement when you first realized that you had the divine power to cause life to come into existence just by the mere thought of it? Well, you still have that power today, even to whom we call the poor. It is just that you have forgotten who you are at your quantum level and who you are serving. When your spirit asked the question, "Who am I?", your "divine natural attribute (DNA)" neutralized energy burst into an incredible brilliance of self-love, self-wonderment, and a desire to express itself through you as it had never known before. Therefore, "do it for the self first" goes against all that is taught by religion and their narrative of how the stories were written about Jesus and the old prophets.

There are many stories where the Master's primary concern was not about serving others first because that is control and interference by a fellow Christ-God-Goddess. Thus, we all have been led to believe by our religions, family, spiritual groups, and educators that salvation comes to us by serving others first before ourselves. This is shown in many ways, like giving money to our churches and organizations for good causes until it hurts, and all that we are doing is feeding the dark side of our consciousness to be lazy.

In fact, this self-sacrificing became the model for all that seemed to be righteous in deserving of God's blessings, when, in fact, we were feeding the dark side of our consciousness the energy needed to give manifestation to what we chose to experience. We need to remember that the Christ within us needs no blessing, as it knows that the aspect of the self is just playing a game of make-believe to learn wisdom.

However, it is not about self-sacrifice either! It is about being clear with our acts in consciousness. Thus, demonstrating balanced and aligned energy where we are not afraid of having abundance, being healthy, and getting ourselves working from an expansional consciousness, and not just from a reality that is only seen as a three-dimensional consciousness, but with a fifth-dimensional quantum consciousness.

When you are clear with your purpose of being a Christ first and foremost, that is when everything changes because of the divine neutralized energy (DNA) that you are feeding your mind and ego on a quantum level. If you are broken down with an illness, being financially exhausted because of job loss, and feeling sorry for yourself, then where is the Master or the King of your Dominion that is your consciousness? It is about others around you witnessing your Mastership in action that sets the example for them to become free, healthy, joyful, and abundant.

It is not about you having the responsibility to serve them first by keeping them healthy, giving them money, and assuring them of heaven after death. That is their responsibility as a Christ unto themselves. You, all of us, are gifted by your Christ spirit with the "free will" to choose anything you desire to experience, and that means anything, good, bad, or neutral, because you, at your core, are a sovereign divine being that has the divine power to act in consciousness.

There is nothing in the heavens that says that we have to fix or repair someone, which would be dishonoring their free will and their divinity to choose and experience their choices anyway. Therefore, the greatest gift that we can do for others is to honor, have compassion, and allow them to experience their choices. Of course, we can help them once they call out to us to understand their choices. But be sure not to help someone that never called out or asked for your help. If you feel that you would like to say something of a divine nature, please do, but allow them to do with it as they please without your interference.

In other words, when one is asking and ready for a teacher to appear, one will. Otherwise, if one is not asking, then the teacher should not interfere. Look at the churches and evangelists and how they try to convert one to Jesus or God, and all they are trying to do is convert one to the dark forces. Has that brought peace to the world and fed the poor? Has it solved the world's problems by pushing their will and their idea of a God on us? I don't believe so! However, if we could understand who God, Christ, and the Goddess are, that would truly change the energy around us, thus the world around us.

Know that an awakened soul understands that all energies serve them, and that is why each of us created our own energy. Therefore, energy exists in a wide variety of frequencies and in many dimensional realms. And it is stored in various types of frequency, such as (i) earth, (ii) cosmic, (iii) crystal, and (iv) the "field" of neutralized quantum energy, all waiting to serve every one of us on many different frequency levels. The best thing for you is to awaken to this; thus, you will always know that you will never have to call in energy to serve them because all that needs to be known and done is allow energy to come in to serve you.

When this is understood from a quantum level, then there is no need to steal energy from others. Also, an awakened soul makes choices without being afraid of the choice, no matter right or wrong. Awakened souls are not afraid to look different, act differently, and believe differently because they know that people have been programmed not to make choices but to think they made choices, which causes them to follow what the dark forces taught them.

For example, our politicians and religions reflect our choices outward as an individual and as a group. And when an individual knows that one is God, Christ, and the Goddess, they understand that they are self-contained sovereign beings who do not need to steal energy or seek help from anywhere outside of themselves. It is better to learn and study who one is first before serving those who are ill or need help. And, that is when one will know how to serve another.

It comes down to loving everyone with having nothing but compassion, unconditional love, and forgiveness for yourself and all those that have trespassed against you without thinking twice about it. That is what is meant by giving and serving others and not by giving them money and love that comes with conditions. Remember, an awakened master in knowing one is Christ makes choices without being afraid they will upset somebody else because it may cause some ripple in others' programming. Also, a master understands not to control the choice made but to allow it to unfold in the direction that gives them the freedom to experience the choice unrestricted.

Most people believe they are making choices, but they are just following what they believe about themselves. Therefore, no choice is made! And since we reflect our choices outward toward others, then know that suffering comes from the lack of "making choices." Instead, we follow others' choices as our means for truth, abundance, health, and safety.

Everything we need is within us, but because of our basic human principles and how we are trained to believe everything comes from outside of us, we pray and serve others from a mind that only understands itself on an emotional level, and with the perception that everything is based on right and wrong, good and bad, light and dark.

Chapter 17

MEMORIES

Without memory, our lives would be incredibly challenging and dangerous, if not impossible. According to the channeled material from the Masters, memory is not only stored in the brain from each lifetime, it is also stored in our heart and throughout the entire celled body. When we look at ourselves in the mirror, we are looking at a body of trillions of cells, and those cells are like living emotional beings with their own memories and lifespan. Not only that, but these cells also have their purpose.

Our physical body cells die as fast as new ones take their place, just like we die here on earth. And like our cells, we have multiple ego-personality aspects of ourselves that die, and others take their place as new incarnations. And like our many ego-personality lifetime aspects, our cells are like a major network, interacting with each other as if it is a major city, and our incarnations are an example of this network.

Therefore, the life we are in now can tap into those past and future lifetime aspects of ourselves and learn the wisdom behind what we have experienced in that life. And like we humans do here on earth with our family DNA, we're born, die, and then pass on our DNA to our family members. And this goes on and on lifetime after lifetime, until we learn to change our DNA to reaching a quantum level. Thus, changing our cellular memories to where we can change our experiences from having poor health to having good health. That is when our diseases, hardships, and karma disappear!

This means every cell in our human body carries the same DNA as our family ancestors. Now, why do Jesus and the Ascended Masters say this? It is because we are our ancestors, and the cells that have died with our physical bodies are just taken up in a new physical body. This is why sons and daughters look like their ancestors or parents and display similar behavior patterns that can carry on their diseases (karma).

The only time we may not do this is when someone is about to leave the family vibrational tree or the DNA pattern because of ending their karma with them. Therefore, cells, like people, have memory! And memory is indestructible, even if our mind has forgotten something. Our body remembers because of our cell's DNA being carried forward into new physical bodies, which means memory is never lost! And this is also why I have the memory of being Peter, the disciple of Jesus. This is also why the masters said in the previous chapter that our memory of knowing "all that we are and ever have been" is there in consciousness. It is that we just have to be awakened to it, and no teaching will ever get us there.

Memory is about helping us understand and become aware that our cells, like our many past lifetimes, have been carrying our life history ever since our consciousness began to create our biography eons ago. In fact, Jesus and the ascended masters look at our cells as the Akashic Records because everything we think, express, choose, and manifest to experience is recorded in our memories' DNA signature. Through memory, we can recall any lifetime, along with recalling our true identity as a God, a Goddess, and as a Christ.

When our focus moved from our Christ consciousness in the beginning stages to a mental consciousness of imaging, it came in with a twist where our consciousness was built on a holographic counterpart of the original. Thus, producing a positive and negative rotational spiral. And with that mental rotational spiral, it produced a photographic memory of all that the mental consciousness acted on, positive and negative. You know the story, "God created man and woman in his image," exact likeness (Genesis 1:27). In other words, consciousness mimics consciousness, and energy mimics energy. Quite simple, isn't it!

Remember, there is only consciousness! We are only consciousness, as energy was created by consciousness. Therefore, in the beginning stages of creating our hologramic mental consciousness, we had no memories or agenda, and therefore, we had no faults, no sins, or reckoning of any wrongdoings. However, once we manipulated the Crystalline pure energy of light and had it appear as Crystal, Cosmic, and Earth Energy, we contaminated these three energies to appear as something separate from the Crystalline Energy. Thus, we created the illusion of polarity or opposition energy that finally led to a belief in power, judgment, and limitations. And that is when we exposed ourselves by trying to dominate others.

It was when, in our "dominating of others" eons ago, that we agreed to a belief in good and evil, right and wrong, judgment, power, limitation, and weakness that began our journey of creating memories of all that we consider as not remembering today. Even the memory of not knowing who we truly are and yet, from our core quantum level, the memory of being the King of our Dominion (consciousness) still lives within us. However, it was necessary to have this experience because if we were going to move away from our Christ consciousness awareness of being the King, we needed something that would remind us later about who we are at our quantum level.

Therefore, we placed in memory the "law of cause and effect" (karma) and the belief in an evil spirit (Satan) that would take us on a journey of discovery. Whatever we thought, believed, or acted upon with this opposing hologramic mental consciousness and dual-energy, it became part of our soul memories as feeling real. Thus, in time, those memories of opposites became our reality to experience in the flesh as something real, and yet it was all an illusion.

Jesus and the Ascended Masters call these memories the Book of Life, also known as the Akashic Records. Everything that we do, good and evil in the now moment or have done in past lifetimes, including everything we think and feel in our heart, is part of our memory being played out here on earth. Therefore, we cannot escape from what we have ever thought, judged, or done, even when we look into "the seven angels" in Revelation 1:20, as it shows that the one who shouted the loudest was the influential forces between our outer ego physical Cain consciousness and our inner mental subconsciousness of record and responsibility.

And this is indicated by the division of the right and left-brain hemispheres, where there is no direct communication between the two other than through memory. Therefore, no man or woman, including Jesus, other than self, is worthy to open the seals of our own memories (Book of Life) until we are ready to awaken to our own Christ consciousness, like our brother Jesus did. No human or religion, not even you, can ever be worthy to open the seven seals portrayed in the Book of Revelation unless you, yourself, overcome the emotional belief that a hologramic God (dual-energy) outside of you created you, judges you, and that you must worship. Why would you want to worship a hologram as a God?

As long as you continue to believe that Jesus is coming for your salvation, then you will never be worthy to open your memories to all that you are as a Christ, including the knowing of your many past lifetimes. No one can save you but yourself because everything must be met on an individual scale, via through memory. Not even "free will" is strong enough to free you from your bondage playing with polarity energy. Why? Because your "free will" is joined with your emotional and mental level of understanding of who Christ is and who you are.

Since it was your masculine side of the mind (Adam) that began appropriating the idea of two powers, positive and negative, and not your feminine soul side of that same mind (individual), then the result was that your mind-soul, since they are one, fell away from its true spiritual nature of "oneness of energy and consciousness" and fell into a belief of two opposing energies as being real instead of seeing it as an illusion to play and learn wisdom.

In other words, and I mentioned this before, once we split our oneness of consciousness and energy to an opposing consciousness and energy, we began to believe in duality, positive and negative, light and dark, good and evil, as something natural. And from this belief, we created the idea of a God who created us and a Satan after our soul, and that is when the masculine side of our mind (man) ignored the feminine soul side of that same mind (woman) as less important.

And we can see this in our world today by men looking at the female population as less important than a man.

Just look how our religions look at women? As the male species control most all aspects of religion. Instead of our masculine side of the mind honoring its feminine soul side as the side that holds our memories, and therefore our salvation, the masculine side of self focuses on its intelligence, free will, and choice as the all-powerful stand-in for our Christ consciousness. Thus, naming itself as the King, Ruler, Master, and the God over all that is created, including woman.

The story of God, Adam, Eve, and the Serpent in the Garden is, therefore, a metaphoric myth that helps us understand our three-dimensional consciousness and why the earth became a place of density to play out our beliefs in a God that is a false God and a Devil that is evil. And what makes this illusion strong is this three-dimensional consciousness of ours, as (i) "I AM" a Christ consciousness, (ii) I work out of a mind-soul, and (iii) I experience life from an ego level, incarnating into many ego-personalities playing with polarity energy to learn wisdom and responsibility for my choices, and to answer the question, "Who am I?"

The name Eve symbolizes feeling, life, and expression and represents our soul region of responsibility for our mind's masculine mental side in choosing what to believe and bring forward to experience. Thus, in any lifetime (male or female), this gives us souled beings the feeling of existence. Our Eve soul side of consciousness (subconsciousness) is only responsible for recording in memory everything that our mind (the masculine) chooses to experience as its reality. Therefore, our mind, the masculine side, is the author and writer of whatever we act on in consciousness to experience outwardly in a flesh body.

And, if your masculine side of the mind consistently believes in good (light) and evil (dark), then you are continually feeding beliefs to your soul consciousness of responsibility to the effect that you will experience these polarized beliefs in the physical, either in this lifetime or in a future lifetime. The covenant we made with God is symbolic of us making a covenant with our own Christ spirit, promising ourselves that we will eventually purify and balance our mind-soul and ego through choice, experiencing, and that of karma. And then, we will integrate all that we are as "one body of consciousness."

We have forgotten about these vows that we took in many past lifetimes to a God outside of us, and now those vows have inhibited us from becoming awakened to our Christ consciousness, all because of feeling guilty about those vows. We have taken vows of poverty, suffering, servitude, and such, trying to justify what we feel as our sinful ways. However, the time has come to get over any guilt that we believe we have and move beyond that deeply embedded shame within our soul side of the mind by letting go of those vows.

To negate all contracts that we have had with our other lifetime aspects and to a false God that we thought was real is to know that our Christ consciousness has kept its promise not to interfere with our mental photographic and opposing creations since we left higher consciousness. And now, the time has come for us to release our Christ spirit from that promise because we have experienced a full range of choices, both good and bad. And once the promise is released, we all come to where we can choose to release our emotional stand when it comes to the belief in sin.

Thus, releasing those memories of our old vows, promises, and rituals, as we understand them now, as only an illusion to be played out in the flesh to have it feel real for our Christ spirit to learn the wisdom of our choices. And, like Jesus before us, we too will be able to take ourselves off the cross of karma and reinstate (resurrect) ourselves as a Christ again. And, this is all done through memory and not done by some religion teaching us about a false god!

Religions proclaim that we are sinners! However, in the eyes of Jesus and the Ascended Masters, we are not and never have been. However, we are a soul that must take full responsibility for our creations, because after all, we are a Christ and the creator of them, and we all have accepted our soul record of memory (Eve) as part of our divinity and our masculine side of the mind. And, since our ego-personality of destruction has no authority, as that belongs to our mind, it is the part of us that must incarnate into the physical body to play out our choices.

Therefore, all physical life on earth, and what we believe is karma, is by way of our Cain consciousness riding the rails of our choices, good and bad. In other words, we are experiencing a three-dimensional consciousness on earth, even though we are multidimensional beings. And our Cain ego-personality consciousness is what experiences the sowing and reaping. Why? Because that was the consciousness that persuaded and fooled our mind-soul into believing we could become like God instead of us knowing that we are already God. In other words, we confront the beast (our ego-personality) and the Anti-Christ (our mind-soul) every second of the day without realizing it.

No wonder we try to avoid taking responsibility for our actions because we are so afraid of the light and more so the dark. Our mind-soul is nothing more than us feeding our ego with so much fear we seem to end up fighting as hard as we can against our own Christ consciousness. Hence, as I did as Disciple Peter in Jesus' day, I also did in this lifetime for a brief moment, but this time I allowed the Christ within me to come forward as Jesus did in his lifetime.

Because of our fear of letting go of our deep-seated memories regarding our dual belief systems, we allow our unawakened mind (the Anti-Christ) to support the beast (ego) in its effort to maintain its control and power over our total consciousness, thus hiding from us, our Christ consciousness. Why do you think Jesus battled with his ego-consciousness (Satan) in the desert before his ego, feeling separate, finally understood that it was part of the wholeness of his divine consciousness? Once Jesus understood from the ego level that he and his mind-soul and ego are of the oneness of the Christ consciousness, that is when he integrated every aspect of his many ego consciousnesses as being "one body of consciousness. Thus, becoming a Christ in his own right!

Therefore, it takes the evolution of our ego personality consciousness moving through the lower energy frequencies for what the *"seven horns"* symbolize in Revelation 5:6, as in initiating many ego-personality incarnations to help us become awakened to this understanding of the Christ consciousness. And once we learn to *"receive the scroll"* mentioned in Revelation 5:7 as the opening of our soul memories, that is when we will awaken and realize that we, our mind-soul and ego in the flesh, have been the sacrificial lamb all along.

This then activates the remembrance of our soul's memories and activities in the way we played them out in each lifetime. And once we transform our ego-personality consciousness of today to being aware of this procedure and into a knowing that our many lifetimes on earth are part of the Christ, we then, in the flesh, can shift our ego-consciousness in the twinkling of an eye to a consciousness of knowing that we are a multi-dimensional being and that our core consciousness is the Christ we seek.

Once we move our focus from the belief that we are separate from our Christ consciousness, we will open up to the hologramic energy of two as an illusion. And that is also when we will transform our outer beastly ego-personality to a whole new unconditional reality, without judgment, where we can tap into full memory of who we truly are from a quantum level, a Christ in our own right. In other words, the redemption of our Cain consciousness.

Know that our soul's feminine side of the mind has carried the memories and lessons of our many past lifetimes to a conscious physical level in this lifetime where we can tap into the wisdom of those experiences. Therefore, only you, not Jesus, can tap into your memories and *"break open the seals"* found in the Book of Revelation, Chapter 6, because it is only you who has paid the price (karma) by accepting and experiencing polarity. Thus, your worthiness to receive the scroll and break open the seven seals refers to you coming into full awareness and knowing that you have the authority as a Christ to tap into all memories from the beginning as to when you recorded them to this now moment.

Therefore, the "seven seals" in the Book of Revelation have nothing to do with religions and their historical interpretations as "plagues" coming to earth. It is more in line with the "plagues" we created and caused within ourselves because of being asleep to whom we are as a Christ. We reflect within what we reflect outward as a reminder of what we are creating as plagues to manifest to experience. This is why we have storms, earthquakes, and many other happenings worldwide because of what we hold within as our beliefs and how we, as a group consciousness, reflect outward.

As said, even our politicians we elect reflect outward what we, as a group consciousness, reflect within ourselves. Therefore, the "seven seals" are about the opening of your soul memories where you quickly learn the wisdom behind the "whys of your suffering." And when you learn how to open up to your soul memories (Akashic Records), that is when you will understand that light and dark, good and bad, right and wrong, come from the same divine pure energy you call the God of light, also known as the Crystalline Energy.

Even though we feel the duality within our creations, the fact remains that it is nothing more than an illusion, a hologram, so we can play and learn about consciousness and how energy works here on earth. We have forgotten that "light" needs the "dark" and vice versa so we can feel and recognize our experiences (plagues), just as a car battery needs positive and negative to start the car. If everything was only of "light" (right), then the quality of us experiencing our choices could never be measured as wisdom.

And if everything were "dark" (wrong), it would all seem without purpose and trivial; thus, feeling inconsequential. That is why both "light" (Jesus) and "dark" (Devil) work together to bring balance, and not that we should favor one over the other by shouting down the dark or light. It is about seeing everything as neutral and allow compassion and unconditional love to be our guide. When we deny our dark creations as part of our soul memories, we suffocate any spiritual understanding and growth. Thus, bringing us more imbalance and stuck energy to work out in the physical as plagues (sins).

How can we heal, bring in riches, or have great relationships if we continuously see ourselves and others only as good and evil without understanding the dark and the light side of ourselves as being part of our total consciousness? When we run from ourselves and the Christ that we are, we lose the opportunity to become balanced and awakened.

Because of our many trials and tribulations journeying through the fire of justice (dual-energy) lifetime after lifetime, our memories have come to serve us well in learning the wisdom behind our choices. And to confirm this, as within our Christ consciousness (symbolized by the *"white horse"* in Revelation 6:1-2), the *"rider with the bow"* is us humans having the courage to reshape and expand our consciousness beyond the mental and physical belief in separation, which is symbolized by the *"first seal"* in Revelation 6:1.

In other words, the *"first seal"* revealed in Revelation, Chapter 6, has to do with the belief about feeling "separated" from our Christ spirit (divinity). The *"second seal,"* revealed in Revelation, Chapter 6, is linked to "self-awareness" and the idea to open up to the memory of you being a Christ also. The *"third seal"* in Revelation, Chapter 6, not only relates to polarity or dual-energy; it also correlates to the belief in a *"Satan character."*

Satan is simply energy (power) created and formed by an individual or the mass human consciousness in the belief that Satan is real and evil. However, the belief in Satan is what makes him real, as evidenced in what we experience every day. And when we, as the Lamb (an ego aspect) of our Christ spirit, broke open the *"fourth seal,"* we took on the "belief in sin" about what we have created in the realm of polarity energy, both physical and non-physical. And since we removed ourselves from our Christ consciousness in favor of a hologramic mental consciousness that expresses and creates opposites, we have been carrying a lot of shame and guilt for what we have created. Therefore, the *"fourth seal"* has to do with us humans taking on a firm belief in "sin."

And when we look into the *"fifth seal"* in Revelation, Chapter 6, the ascended masters are speaking of "letting go of our suffering (karma)." We all have the capability and the means to transform our stubborn ego-personality consciousness and become a witness to all of our underlying lifetime personalities where we have played with the forces of the light and dark (polarity energies) as if they are real.

And when Jesus and the Ascended Masters speak of the *"sixth seal"* in Revelation, Chapter 6, it is the belief that you need rescuing and, therefore, "salvation." It will not be Jesus and his army of angels, and not even a spaceship, that will come to save you from the Beast (all those that work against one being Christ) because you are the only one that can rescue yourself from your many "ego-personalities" of the past and future. Therefore, if you happen to see a Jesus individual coming from behind the clouds, then know that it is a false Jesus, created by the dark forces to fool you and to steal your energy and soul.

To keep you captured in an energy stealing situation. Do not be fooled! It is just the dark forces creating a situation to trap those of religious faith into following their plan to control you. Know that you are the Christ and the Lord King, and therefore salvation is within you already. Salvation comes as soon as you see through your dogmatic memories and beliefs that are tied to a false god and a false Jesus as to coming to earth to save you.

Also, as per Jesus's message here in this book, there is no need to worship him to achieve ascension because we are already part of this ascension once we awaken to the core essence of being a Christ already. Salvation and ascension have always been part of our total consciousness here on earth, no matter where we are in life. Again, it is just that we need to awaken to the real truth about Christ, God, and the Goddess, not being part of any religion. It is just you!

However, according to Jesus and the Ascended Masters, the *"sixth seal"* is where ninety-seven percent of the population is today, as most refuse to let go of their belief in dual-energy (light and dark), a God and a Jesus on a cross that belongs to religion, and that they are only human. Because of the mass consciousness's strong belief in dual-energy and that we are a three-dimensional consciousness, the *"sixth seal"* will remain closed until one realizes that they are multidimensional and a Christ also. Therefore, how many lifetimes will it take you to look into your emotions regarding this false god, dual-energy beliefs, and that Jesus will appear from out of the sky someday to save you?

The answer is simple. It will take as long as it takes for you to understand the *"seventh seal"* in Revelation 8:1 as it is all about the "silencing of your mind" when making choices to be manifested to experience. From the time we all left our Christ consciousness, we have chosen to experience polarity energy. And now, the opportunity has presented itself where we can open the "seventh seal" just by the "silencing of our mind," close our eyes, and then do some deep breathing before any "consciousness act."

This act is with our pituitary gland and is symbolic for the Church of Laodicea. As the opening of the *"seventh seal"* grants the seven angels (Endocrine System) to sound off in unison, allowing us to come into "self-governing Kingship" (a sovereign God-Goddess in our own right) and in alignment to "all that we are at our core" as opposed to others ruling over us. The *"seventh seal"* is not only the unfolding of the mystery of the Apocalypse, but it also uncovers the mystery behind Christ's return to earth as you.

However, as Jesus mentioned to me, our inflexible nature will keep some of you asleep to the real truth because of your incredible ties to your emotions, religion, and institutional group consciousness. From the works of Geoffrey Hoppe, Crimson Circle, I read a Shoud where Tobias mentions, and I quote. "The 'seventh seal' is the butterfly (us humans) leaving the effectiveness of the cocoon (three-dimensional consciousness), which has hidden our true identity for eons of time."

My friends, we have forgotten that the *"seventh seal"* has been part of our consciousness since we left our higher quantum consciousness (the first creation) eons ago. And now, because of our many lifetimes sowing and reaping (bearing our cross), we have the potential to move from the third and the fourth dimension to the fifth-dimensional consciousness if we so choose. And yes, I have heard the phrase "fourth density," but let it be known that the "fourth density" is the same as one moving into the "fifth dimension."

Also, know that the Rapture that everyone has been waiting for is indeed upon you and is waiting for your awakening from a three-dimensional consciousness to a fifth-dimensional consciousness. So, are you ready to let go of all that you have believed since the time you were born here on earth? It is your choice!

Chapter 18

LEARN HOW TO REMOVE YOUR CHAINS

How do we remove our chains from the control and slavery we have placed on ourselves since birth? We do it by becoming conscious creators and let all that we have learned from our churches, governments, teachers, friends, and even our parents go! Remember, every one of us is a Christ and the true God and Goddess in our own right, having no one above or below us that is more holy and powerful. And by accepting that we are responsible for everything that comes into our lives, with no exceptions, not even the excuse of being born poor, rich, sexually abused, or beaten.

We must accept the responsibility for whatever we are experiencing right now, for we are the creator of it all. We cannot be a conscious creator or a true master, like Jesus, if we are still blaming ourselves, others around us, or circumstances for what happens to us in life, even if we believe it is not our fault. So, why do the Ascended Masters say this? They say it because somewhere in some lifetime past, we have chosen to experience what we are experiencing today, even though we cannot remember.

Accepting the truth about you having different incarnations becomes the first step toward healing. Think about feeling something that touches you about yourself but not accepting it because of fear. This is where you learned to blame others for your misfortunes in life. Look how society, like the poor, blames the rich, or how we blame our parents, our schools, and our politicians, not realizing they represent something within ourselves that need working on; otherwise, we would not have voted for them.

We fail to look at what we have chosen to experience from a deeper level to understand ourselves as spiritual beings. We even chose the country where we need to be born and our parents and those who will be our friends to meet what we want to accomplish in a particular life. It is not about blame or what is right or wrong when it comes to our true identity because our Christ consciousness only looks at our experiences as a route to grow in wisdom and in consciousness.

We can find souls everywhere that went through some very dark times feeling alone and betrayed by a friend, family, a neighbor, a business associate, and even God. And yet, it is all part of everyone's divine plan to learn wisdom and become a conscious creator. Know that we are in creatorship training, and we have been doing it in many various ways using multi-dimensional realms and creating many human ego-personality clones of ourselves in fulfilling that divine plan. It is just the earth realm of dual-energy becoming a dimension where we can experience very harsh realities.

However, the time has come for us to forgive ourselves, forgive others, and learn to trust and love ourselves as a human and as a Christ also. Know that earth and dual-energy (good and evil) are the last steps before going on into the third circle of no-suffering, and yet, to get to this no-suffering (no karma), we must learn to let go of our story, who we believe we are as a human, and what we believed happened to us as far as our freedom.

This is represented by the 1000 years of peace mentioned in the Book of Revelation. The number "one" (1) represents you coming into integrating "all that you are and ever have been" since the time you have been journeying through cycles of mental and physical incarnations, as it represents the two first zero. The third zero represents you moving, once awakened to whom you truly are from the quantum level, a Christ in your own right that is now free to choose a cycle of no pain and suffering.

It is not about being at fault either or about your belief systems and your faith. It is about your desire to know who you are as a divine being. And therefore, it is about taking responsibility for your choices and your creations. It is also about the experiences that you took from every different direction to understand how dual-energy works with the belief in power. In the end, you learn who you are from a fifth-dimensional consciousness.

Know that we all truly embodied our chosen creations of duality and the power that came with it that brought our creations to life and then have it feel so real that we got lost in it. However, also know that we carry the wisdom of all those opposing experiences and the meaning of how power played a big part in what we experienced. Therefore, the time has come for us to look at who we truly are from a fifth-dimensional consciousness and accept full responsibility as the creator and not as if there is a creator above us or that someone will come and save us from the Anti-Christ.

When we do this, we are going to find ourselves knocking at the door of our own Christ consciousness to unify all parts and pieces of ourselves that are spread throughout many dimensions. And as these fragments or aspects of ourselves may feel confused, angry, and frustrated, it is due to them feeling left out when it comes to us, in this lifetime, ignoring them. Understand, before our past lifetime choices and experiences can accept our Oversoul as their creator, we have to accept our Christ spirit, as to whom we indeed are at our core. Otherwise, these fragments of ourselves will remain part of the false god.

It is not about our excuses or the words we come up with to justify what we are experiencing or feeling emotionally. It is about accepting no more "what if's," or "but I was" excuses, or "being unworthy" of having a meaningful life. Every ego-personality aspect of you wants to come back home to the real you, the higher quantum consciousness part of you. And if you are not clear to who you indeed are, a Christ in your own right, then it will be challenging to move to a higher frequency fifth-dimensional consciousness when you have aspects of yourself still fighting you.

If you haven't totally accepted your own Christ consciousness as your Oversoul, then all I can say is to expect your accidents, ups and downs, dramas, and your life crisis to continue in a three-dimensional world. Do not expect your cross on the wall or around your neck to save you because you will wait a long time. Remember, Jesus already experienced his time on earth and left this three-dimensional world and therefore is not coming back to save us, as he already helped us remember who we are at our core essence. It is now up to each of us to grow in spirit and awaken ourselves to the real truth.

However, Jesus and the ascended masters want you to know that you are loved dearly by your own Christ spirit even if you do not go to church, help your neighbor, or love a false God outside of you. So, step outside of your belief systems, take responsibility for yourself and become a conscious creator, good, bad, past, and present. Once this is done, then all your ego-personality aspects (other lifetimes) will feel your love for them. Thus, you create an avenue for them to come home to their creator, you.

Remember an awakened master will always take responsibility for him/herself and not for anyone else's life choices, even if it is a spouse, father, mother, son or daughter, brother or sister, a grandchild or friend, or even a foe feeling obligated or guilty because of faith, duty, or honor. It is not about faith, duty, honor, or praying to God for their healing and guidance. It is that you cannot be their co-creator because you "know not what they have chosen" from the soul level to find their own balance.

Learn to understand the bigger picture as to what is going on in their lives. And yes, it is okay to show your love for them but do it because you choose not to feel obligated to do so. Everyone on earth uses dual-energy as their source, and therefore we work with sin and karma daily. However, know that life is fair, even if we don't think so! Know that life is perfect because we are perfect. Aren't we choosing what experiences we want to experience? There will always be obstacles and limitations to challenge us on an emotional level. However, it is how we accept these challenges that separate us from receiving a higher energy frequency that will pull us over the top in reconnecting us to our Christ consciousness for healing and guidance.

Receiving miracles in our life is about commitment from our heart center that we are indeed the creator of our lives and the world we live in today, and not about some God above us who created us as good and evil. It is not about someone who owes us for something, not even a living. Everyone, rich, poor, sick, or healthy, is equal in God's eyes and therefore connected to the same opportunities and potentials just by being divine.

When you sign your proclamation that you will take full responsibility for yourself and that you are the creator of your world, watch what happens. You will automatically begin to create miracles for yourself because you understand that you are not a victim but are a true creator. And if you acknowledge your own divine creatorship authority, you will bring into your life completion (knowing one is Christ). Remember, Jesus did not blame anyone for his crucifixion, as the word "crucifixion" means "taking responsibility for your acts in consciousness."

When you realize that you have nothing to fix about yourself because of sin, karma, shame, or guilt, that is when you will begin to create the miracles of abundance, health, joy, and a knowing that you no longer have to fear God, Satan, or any control over your life. We all first must realize that God is not the God we believe him be. God is about coming into a realization that we are God (pure neutral energy), we are Christ (Oversoul), and we are the Goddess (the I AM) in human form instead of trying to preserve our human identity as who we believe we are from an emotional level.

When we learn to let go of all our controls, especially the control of what is right and wrong, needing salvation, and that we need a lot of money to feel safe, our divine inner knowingness can become synchronistic with our outer human consciousness. The more we try to control things in our life, the more restrictive and limiting we become. And the last one to know this is our human ego with all of its emotions and needless claims that someone owes us a living or an apology.

Chapter 19

THE BIG LIE!

I have encountered and received numerous dreams and visions in my life that have come from the angelic realm. And I would like to share a particular dream that tells the story about our real home. And it is not the earth! When Jesus mentioned that he was not of this world (John 18:36), it also applies to all humans here on earth. Earth is just a temporary place to learn the wisdom of our choices. Especially the choice to believe COVID 19 and many illnesses are real. Sometimes we humans, out of fear, of course, never look at what makes common sense anymore.

Here is an example. You walk into a restaurant without a mask on your face because of COVID 19, if that still applies today, so the host tells you that you must put the mask on until you get to your table, and then you can take it off. I even have heard where the government is thinking of having us wear noise masks when we eat. How will the virus know not to attack you when you are sitting at your table eating? I guess it will only attach when you are walking to the table. This is what I mean by common sense. And as you know, there are many examples like that. Anyway, let's get back to my dreams and visions.

Over sixteen years ago, I dreamt where I was standing in the kitchen of the home in Maine where I was born. And yes, I was not born in a hospital. I was born in the home that I lived in my first eighteen years of life. Anyway, in my dream, I was standing in the kitchen area next to the table where I remember eating many meals, facing and looking into the bedroom where I slept as a child. My childhood bedroom was right off the kitchen. Suddenly, I saw a tall bearded man standing there looking out at me from the bedroom. And from what I saw, this bearded man appeared to be dressing for a special occasion.

That is when I felt an overwhelming urge to walk toward my bedroom door to enter, and to my surprise, this bearded man was Jesus. Of course, my thoughts moved to, "What was Jesus doing in my bedroom where I slept as a child?" Also remember, this is the same bedroom where I was first introduced to Jesus and Mother Mary as a child. From my dream, I was sensing that Jesus was dressing for a special occasion. And it was confirmed because, intuitively, I felt that he was preparing himself to come and address the world once again.

The amazing part of this dream was why was Jesus preparing himself in the bedroom that I slept in for so many years? One would think that Jesus would have better places to prepare himself for such an occasion. As I saw Jesus working on himself to address the world, that is when I walked into the bedroom to greet him. And when I did, I found myself stopping about three feet in front of him. That was when Jesus greeted me, saying, *"Hi Terry, do you need any money?"* And my reply to Jesus was, "No"! And yet, right after saying "no," I followed up with, "All that I need is a hug."

In response, Jesus walked up to me and put his arms around me, and gave me a big hug. Once the hug was over, Jesus looked me in the eyes, saying, *"Terry, you have the knowledge, the understanding, and the wisdom to make yourself clear about how people on earth live in their illusions, and all that you have to do is let it out."* After hearing this come from Jesus, not only did I thank him for having confidence in me, I quickly added and said to him, "If you (Jesus) enter the world, people again would not recognize or accept you as Christ, so why bother?"

However, even though saying this to Jesus, his reply back to me was: *"You are right, most of the world's population would not recognize me at all, but it is something that has to be done."* Right after his comment, Jesus then smiled at me and then walked out of the bedroom, leaving me watching him fade away. That is when I found myself alone in my childhood bedroom, not wearing a shirt. And yes, I found this weird because when Jesus was with me, I did have on a shirt. But, once Jesus was gone, I found myself shirtless.

So, why now, after he leaves, I seemed to lost my shirt? I remember vividly being puzzled about it in my dream also. So, my first reaction was to find a shirt. And, as one would know when it comes to dreams, I suddenly found one hanging there in the bedroom! But I somehow felt that the shirt was not mine, that it belonged to someone else.

Nonetheless, I also felt that I knew the person that the shirt belonged to, and therefore, without his permission, I decided to borrow the shirt and put it on. But, to my surprise, once I put the shirt on, as it did fit, I then saw the person who owned the shirt come right into the bedroom where I was standing. Again, to my surprise, as he entered, he did not recognize the shirt, so I said nothing about it. It was then that we both walked out of my childhood bedroom and proceeded to walk to school together. And once we both arrived and entered the school building, we decided to enter the cafeteria to eat. However, as we walked into the cafeteria, we both found it a big mess. And as we both stood and stared at this mess, I observed the school principal getting ready to address everyone, including myself and the person with me.

Then I heard the principal announce that we were the blame for the cafeteria's condition being a mess, and because of it, we were not going to eat that day. That is when the principal took the food trays and rolled them out of the cafeteria. Once the food trays were rolled out, the principal returned to the cafeteria and lectured us about what we did wrong. And what happened next in my dream again took me by surprise.

As the principal was lecturing us about what we did wrong, I noticed that he was looking directly at me. That is when I spoke up, softly at first, and then later, I spoke with authority and confidence, saying to him and everyone in the cafeteria that the principal is lying and that he, himself, was the one that messed up the cafeteria and wanted to blame it on us. That was when the principal looked at me with great annoyance. And when feeling the principal's annoyance, I sensed what happened in the cafeteria was a setup to make us look like we did something wrong, although we did nothing wrong but believed him.

After sensing this, I turned around and left the cafeteria, where I met up with another schoolmate. And as I explained to him what happened in the cafeteria and how we were all misled by the principal with his lies, the schoolmate began to understand precisely what I was speaking about. Because of his understanding, he then began to spread the word to all the other students. I could hear him telling them how we are under a cloud of lies but we are blind to it. That is when I woke up from my dream! And after getting up from bed, I was very puzzled about the many parts of the dream.

First, it was Jesus wanting to come to earth to address the world. Then our discussion, the hug, my shirtless event, and how the dream went on from there. By midday, the night after the dream, my thoughts went to maybe Jesus was actually coming back to Earth to make his appearance once again, just like the Bible predicted. However, right after thinking this, my intuitive feelings directed me to write the dream down and place it with my other dreams and visions to be looked at in the future. And, here I am now, writing this book and coming face to face with the dream notes of what I wrote down many years prior.

And as I read my notes on the dream, I began to receive messages on its interpretation. Therefore, I decided to include it in this book. However, I found that the dream was not about Jesus getting ready to come to earth to address the world but was about preparing myself to come to earth to address the world as a disciple of my own Christ Consciousness. Hence, Jesus, the Christ, represents the Christ consciousness within me, as he also represents the Christ consciousness within all of us. But we are asleep to it!

When I found myself in the home where I was born as a child in Maine, it symbolizes myself as a Christ awakened before even coming into this lifetime as Terry. And when Jesus asked about "needing money," and my reply was "no," it means that when I came into this lifetime as the personality aspect named Terry, and the one who owns the shirt (physical body), I will have plenty of energy (money) to accomplish my mission. And once I deliver the divine message to the mass consciousness about "we are not who we believe we are" and how we are living in a world of darkness, that will be the time when I become fully emerged with the Christ consciousness within myself, thus, becoming "one body of consciousness," as in, so it was in the beginning, so shall it be in the end.

This merging of my Christ consciousness in this lifetime has allowed me to fulfill my mission in all ways, including me never having to come back to earth in another lifetime. In other words, I have risen (raptured), as Jesus did back in his day! To confirm this message was when Jesus said to me: *"Terry, you have the knowledge, the understanding, and the wisdom to make yourself clear about how people on earth live their illusions, and all that you have to do is let it out."* Therefore, as Jesus did as a Christ over two thousand years ago, I have done the same in this lifetime with the writing of my books.

The home I was born in and slept in as a child represents the angelic realm, the very place that I learned that I, too, was a Christ in my own right. And the hug given by Jesus represents this, as Christ and I are one and the same! It is the same for everyone else! All that is left for everyone is to awaken to it. And once I put on the shirt, symbolized by my physical body, that was when I incarnated as Terry on earth as a disciple to my own Christ consciousness to address the world by delivering the message to you in the form of books.

And to summarize this message, it is about those who are ready to ascend to the fifth dimension and higher (Heaven on Earth), where you get to learn that you are a Christ also. Thus, leaving behind the old three-dimensional world of pain, suffering, lies, and illusions. The borrowing of the shirt is actually myself in spirit creating a physical body to come to earth (school) to help awaken the mass consciousness (those in the cafeteria) to all the lies and deceptions that are being fed to us by the dark forces, such as our politicians, the media, big businesses, our scholars and educators, and our religions (all represented by the school principal).

As I mentioned earlier, if one experiences or sees a Jesus-like figure that acts in a religious manner or in a dualistic way, then know it comes from religion's God of the Bible. Know that it took the Monks in 1975, Jesus in 2004, the visit by the Ascended Masters in 2004, the Archangels in 2012, and my many dreams and visions before I was awakened to "all that I am as a Christ," and to the lies of those in charge of our lives.

The entering into the cafeteria to eat refers not only to myself in this lifetime but also to those in the physical surrounded by many lies, dogmatic beliefs, and traditions brought on by the institutions of the world's dark forces claiming they know what is best for us. It is religion, and its leaders, the politicians, big businesses, the media, our educators, and many more representing the "principal" that have been feeding us nothing but lies upon lies for many thousands of years with what we wanted to hear. All because of not wanting to take full responsibility for our creations.

Remember, if we are controlled by the dark forces, then we, from a subconsciousness level, have participated by allowing them to control us. And when the school principal came into the cafeteria and observed the mess that he claimed we made, this fortifies how much we are under the influence and control of the world's dark forces. As we eat, think, choose, and carry out the devil's desires without realizing how many lies our world leaders have fed us shows how much we are asleep to the real truth. When one fails to listen to all sides of an issue, one is working out of a consciousness frequency that is stuck instead of allowing one to expand.

We, the people, completely overlook the media, our church leaders, our politicians, and our schools and educators as being the arm for the devil, brainwashing us to believe that they are the way to the light, and therefore must follow them with faith and confidence. They used the words of a false God against us, and we allowed it and followed them without question. My friends, we all have been trapped in a mind and a three-dimensional world where lies and deceit are the norms. Therefore, the dark forces are the ones that have created a mess of this world by filling us with their lies and deceptions that may, if we are not willing to awaken to it, result in a one-world government where everyone is under mind control that leads to the loss of our individuality and freedom.

When the school principal took out the food trays and then came back into the cafeteria to lecture the students (we the people of the earth), this symbolizes how the controlling powers of the dark forces have taught and instructed us to give up our free will and individuality to choose our own spiritual pathway, along with asking questions about why we are so fearful about a system that they created for us to experience.

And here we are, the year 2021, allowing the dark forces to vaccinate us with formulations of unknown origins that could change our DNA to a lower frequency, keeping us locked into a three-dimensional consciousness. And if we do not comply, they will turn off our privileges to travel, buy goods, and food to eat. And when the school principal talked directly to me in the dream, it symbolizes the system and how they want to keep people like me under their control by not publishing books like this one or you reading it.

By the dark forces of the church and their faithful three-dimensional followers knowing that they could lose their power and control over books like this, they will work as hard as they can to discredit these books and all those that are working hard in hopes of awakening others to the real truth from getting out. The principal's direct look at me indicated that not only will I speak out, but many others like me.

Of course, I, and many awakened ones, did begin at first speaking out slowly, which is symbolized by my other published books and what has been published by others in previous years. But now, with this book, and with the help of other awaken souls, divine intervention has occurred as of December 21, 2020, giving me and others complete confidence and the energy to expose the dark forces and their agenda to take over the people of the world.

Jesus said in the New Testament that Christ would one day return to Earth and that many would not recognize him, and here we are in the days of darkness, and very few recognize the Christ consciousness, which is why Jesus said, many would not be ready for the harvest. This means that many upon this earth are not ready to awaken to where one ascends to the fifth dimension or higher because they are unwilling to wake up from their sleep. To these people, compassion is the only word, for they may have to do another twenty-five-thousand-year cycle before it comes around to them again.

We, most people of the world today, are blind to any realization that the Rapture and the Harvest spoken off in the Bible is happening right now, in this now moment. And to my surprise, most of them who are blind to this happening are those of the religious order and their followers, all because of the churches around the world have been placed under the control of the evil forces. Even the Vatican has fully emerged with the dark forces.

To understand that Jesus, the man, in my dream coming back to earth is not about him coming from behind a cloud to be our savior, but it is about some of us moving forward into the fifth dimension. It is about learning how to reconnect ourselves to our own Christ consciousness in this lifetime. For me, I have awakened to my Christ consciousness, and now I have passed that message on to others through this book. So, do not be fooled by some false flag about Jesus coming to earth to save us.

As we understand it, the Rapture happens when we are willing to awaken to receive the Christ and truth within our hearts about who we are at our core and not who we think we are from a materialistic view. My friends, it was with divine intervention in 2004 that helped me speak up, softly at first, but now I speak with confidence and authority because I know that I am a Christ also, and so are you if you are willing to open your heart in recognizing it.

If you are determined to remain in the dark of a three-dimensional world, then be prepared to have many more lifetimes playing on a three-dimensional planet because Earth, as we know it, is going to ascend, like in a Rapture, and move into a fifth-dimensional planet where "heaven on earth" becomes the norm. You know, the Golden age! This is all confirmed by what I experienced as a ten-year-old child when Jesus and Mother Mary introduced themselves to me in my childhood bedroom. And today, I work with them and a group of Ascended Masters in presenting to you this book of messages about the grand awakening moving upon us very fast.

This is also why, for my first forty-six years on earth, I had to experience hypnosis, untruths, deceptions, lies, and cover-ups, and all that was hidden within my own soul before I could discover that the aspect of Terry is a disciple of the Christ Consciousness within himself, as well as, a disciple of Jesus, the Christ when he walked the earth. I am also a priest under the order of Lord Melchizedek.

And here we are today, 2021, and just like in Jesus' day, many people upon the earth still do not recognize Christ's message about the dark forces of the world and how they are still deceiving us into believing in a system where we have been brainwashed into believing they are our keepers when it comes to truth, God, and Christ. And we have blindly followed their lies for a very long time. My friends, we, the people, have been blinded by our belief in a system that only understands money as power and that we are their slaves to do as they please.

These dark-minded souls work hard to steal our energy, and we allow it by voting and keeping them in powerful positions. And these powerful institutions are our church leaders, our politicians, large banks, the media, and large corporate businesses. However, their time here on earth ruling over us is coming to a close because of Earth moving into the fifth dimension. We all have to come to a critical place in our hearts where we need to begin to question the status quo. And, of course, the choice is ours to make if we decide to stay in the dark or move into the light.

It comes to recognizing the media, our religions, big businesses, our educators, the Republicans, Democrats, our Tech Companies, and many of our Generals who have lied and fooled us into believing they are there to watch out for our best interest and all they have done is delivered us into the devil's hand where we do not even recognize truth from lies, or ourselves, our friends, our family, and our neighbors anymore. We seem to be divided into groups where we wear the devil's mask to indicate our allegiance to the dark, and those who refuse to wear the devil's mask indicate that they work for Christ and the truth.

If you happen to be wearing a mask, please allow yourself to take a few deep breaths and feel your fear of the dark forces within and what is being fed to you by the mass media. Of course, take the mask off before you do the deep breathing. Open your eyes and clear away the cotton in your ears so you can hear Christ speaking to you. Look around and learn to reexamine your trust in those that have been steering you away from your awakening (Rapture).

In closing this chapter, I want to leave you with this: My intuition has guided me without fail, and I back up my intuition with my connection to the fifth dimension, the Christ within me, and those Ascended Masters that work with me every day from higher dimensions. I have always felt within my body that there are three different types of consciousness. I feel my (i) <u>mind</u> (head) where logic and reason prevail its truths/lies and its fears, my (ii) <u>heart</u> where my Christ spirit prevails its wisdom according to my soul growth; and I feel within my (iii) <u>belly</u> my emotions rising to a certain point where I need to listen to my fears and how they have controlled every choice I made.

However, since I am aware of these three types of consciousnesses sparling within me, I can feel they must operate in balance before I can truly understand "what are lies and what are truths," especially as complex as to what we see today as this virus unfolding before our very eyes. In other words, (i) logic, judgment, mindset, fear, and attitude will always be dominated by the <u>head</u>. (ii) Unconditional love, compassion, spirit, truth, and light will always be dominated by raw <u>intuition and our heart,</u> and our (iii) <u>emotions</u> will always dominate our choices and our connection to the dark forces that are now being played out around the world.

Therefore, I can only urge you to stay connected to your heart center as that is where, through deep breathing and study, you will recognize the light (truth) from the dark (lies). I say this to help avoid the temptation to retreat into a mental and emotional state of judgment and fear because of our deep-seated beliefs that follow us around in many lifetimes. Allow your heart, intuition, compassion, focus, passion, and love of unconditional means to guide you to what is truth and what are lies.

For example, the mainstream media and the professed science report about a very active virus called COVID 19 and its effect on our health and well-being can be reduced by wearing a mask for protection. And here we are now, and the scientific world wants us to double wear masks, which will significantly reduce our health chances even more. However, when applying deep breathing to this distressing declaration of mask-wearing, one's intuitive consciousness will reveal not only the virus's true intentions but also those that are lying to us about its cure.

When I applied this while deep breathing, I found myself intuitively connected to my Christ consciousness, and that is when it revelated to me that this virus is not what we think it is. In fact, the mainstream media's marketing of the virus is to have us believe that it is real when, in truth, it is nothing but a version of the flu. And those who live in fear and wear the mask are the ones who contract the virus, even though it is not real.

Learn to study things, open your mind, stay in your heart center, and stop taking for granted that the church you belong to, the media you listen to, the educators you pay attention to, and the politicians you hear on television and vote for are telling you the truth. What is being overlooked by those of a three-dimensional world and consciousness is that we, the people, are coming to a fork in the road that leads to higher consciousness (fifth-dimension) or leads us down the same traveled road of darkness that has enveloped this world for the last sixteen thousand years.

The choice is yours, as it is time to awaken from your sleep and allow your Christ consciousness to come in and work with your heart and intuition from the fifth-dimensional consciousness. Know and understand that your Christ consciousness is trying to speak with you through your three-dimensional consciousness. So, why are you ignoring it?

I understand that many may be shocked by this revelation of what I just said here in this book, and it is absolutely normal to feel that way. But, before you write me off as some misguided fool who claims to know Christ first hand, I ask you to feel into your fear, not only of this overblown virus but the anger and the frustrations that come with it. Look around you and see what is happening right before your eyes. Learn to do some self-searching and stop relying on others to feed your mind with what seems to be propaganda.

With self-searching, you will notice right away how much of your freedoms have been taken away by your government ever since 9/11. Know that you are not species capable of staying still and watching the dark forces of this world take more and more of your energy and allowing them to do with you as they please. Know that consciousness is everything, as it takes consciousness to create your beliefs and fears. Know that deep within, you are not wired for the kind of reactions you are playing out in response to a pandemic. And therefore, it is unwise to believe that you can just sit, wait, and degrade yourself, all because of fear, thinking your problems will pass from you so you can go on with normal living. All that you are doing is inviting in more darkness, more lies, and more problems.

What is happening right before your eyes is that the polarity shift between the light and the dark is occurring very rapidly. And you are experiencing the polarity shift right now where the light is taking over the dark, and in its attempt, the dark is working as hard as it can to stop it. This is why you are feeling very confused about what is light and what is dark. We can see this in our past presidential elections, as some believed Mr. "T" was from the dark and Mr. "B" was from the light.

However, don't be deceived because what you may believe is the dark is actually the light working on overcoming the dark. Please note: This does not mean Mr. T or Mr. B is light or dark, as I show this as an example. Remember, the devil is very tricky! The mind is such a place to escape from when dealing with your dark side because it is easier for the mind to bring out its truths as it sees fit in dealing with your beliefs and choices, no matter if right or wrong.

The mind pretends that it is smart and knows things, but in truth, we run away from our dark side, which is why we are running away from what is right in front of us, and we are too proud to admit it. In other words, it is time for you to make a choice, no more sitting on the sidelines. Either you choose darkness or light! We have forgotten that our soul's wisdom comes from memory and what we have experienced in the past, if we want to call it the past.

This is how we grow and expand in consciousness, as the dark side of our creations is reflected right back to us from those of past lifetimes and group consciousness. And as we incarnate lifetime after lifetime, the mind records in memory all our choices and experiences based on our emotional responses to any given situation. This is where our belief systems come from, as it helps us feel our experiences first hand. And this makes us go through endless cycles, lifetime after lifetime, and the saddest thing is when we do this, we forget more and more about who we are at our quantum level.

Thus, we taint the real facts to what actually happened from one lifetime to the next. The mind records it that way and then says to itself, I will pull up memory and feel into what is needed from what I am receiving for information. And if the information received does not correspond to where I am emotionally in consciousness, the mind will pull things in memory with a lot of bias and judgment because the mind will always relate feelings with emotions because of self-protection and wanting to be right. Therefore, the mind leaves out the real truth because of the need to control any given information.

Our mind is conditioned to believe and think that truth is nothing but the truth and that there is no in-between. Therefore, the mind believes that it must fight as hard as it can to uphold in memory to what we have already been taught as our truths. My friends know that our ascension (Rapture) cannot occur until we learn to surrender to our fears and then learn how to overcome them with study, keeping an open mind, doing deep breathing, staying with unconditional love, and understanding that we all were given the right under God to breathe without covering our face to block out our God-given right to fresh air.

When we learn and understand that fear is the route for the dark forces in stealing our energy and our soul, we set ourselves up for a takeover of our consciousness, our divinity, our choices, our beliefs, our energy, and then leaving ourselves as a slave to them.

As humans, we assign our mental consciousness based on what we believe is the foundation of our truths without realizing that it is all based on our emotions. And using energy and consciousness to manifest what we believe are our truths, we then add our emotions, closing out any thought of what we are experiencing that is coming from the dark forces and what they want us to do for them. And wearing a mask to cover our faces is a prime example of their power over us even though we stand as one million to one.

We know this to be true because we see ourselves intellectually and emotionally believing the dark forces when they say it is to protect us and others around us, including our elderly parents. We fail to use common sense because of fear and our emotional thinking when the dark forces say that it is okay to buy goods from a large corporation but not from a family business. It is as if one cannot catch the virus buying goods from a large corporation but somehow catch it if the goods are purchased from a family business.

This hypnosis of the dark side is stronger and more pervasive than ever, which is why we are locked into a consciousness that only sees good as dark and evil as light, the complete opposite. And this is seen with our 2020 presidential elections, as in my opinion, Mr. "T" was seen as the dark and Mr. "B" as the light, and yet it could be the opposite. It is the same with Israel, as Israel's government is of the dark while the Jewish people are of the light. With such a fear warped three-dimensional consciousness, we humans display such reluctance to learn to tap into our intuition and feel the common sense of things instead of automatically geared toward what terrifies us the most.

Thus, we follow and help the dark complete their plan to take over the world at our children's expense. For myself, I look through the eyes of a fifth-dimensional consciousness and higher, and what I see is nothing more than a three-dimensional consciousness filled with separateness and fear. A three-dimensional consciousness that can only see what is emotionally in front of them without having any indication of what is beyond their five physical senses.

Take the date on what occurred in New York City on September 11, 2001, as the date is broken down in numerology ($9 + 1 + 1 + 2 + 0 + 0 + 1 = 14$, where its lowest dominator is $1 + 4 = 5$). According to the Ascended Masters, all that is material living is tied to sacred geometry, as numerology is part of it. Therefore, the number five (5) relates to a three-dimensional world where one is completely using one's five physical senses to make choices instead of moving past their five senses.

In contrast, a fifth-dimensional consciousness operates beyond the mind and its fear-based three-dimensional consciousness and its five physical senses where good and evil exist. A fifth-dimensional consciousness operates with an awareness in life that comes from one's higher senses and their Christ consciousness and not from a mind of good and evil believes. In other words, to embody a fifth-dimensional consciousness, one simply needs to slow down the mind, take deep breaths, and act in consciousness from our authentic Christ consciousness.

And, in doing so, we take part in shaping our mind (the Anti-Christ), our Cain ego of deception, and a consciousness to cooperate and align ourselves to whom we are as a Christ in the making. I can understand why one would be skeptical about a fifth-dimensional consciousness in what still seems like a three-dimensional world filled with fear and corruption, false information, and numerous injustices. However, when we learn to stand up to whom we truly are as a Christ in our own right, then the status quo of fear no longer serves us or the dark forces. That is when we ascend to a higher consciousness, as in a rapture, that knows what will happen once we learn to let go of the old way of thinking.

One more thing, since we are on the subject of lies, Jesus, to whom we call Christ, is not the same person who walked with us as Christ over 2000 years ago. The name "Jesus" comes from the Greeks and those that love power. Yeshua Ben-Joseph comes from the Hebrew man that walked the earth over 2000 years ago. We know this to be true because, during Yeshua's time, the name Jesus never existed during Yeshua's time on earth as a Jew. It is the same way with the name, "GOD," as the dark forces changed the name "Yahweh" to a false "God" (Jehovah, meaning "I AM Your God"), where "Yahweh" is the actual name of God, meaning "I AM That I AM, a God unto myself."

God and Jehovah are names that come from dual-energy beliefs, as it is for the name Jesus. This means the Bible as we know it has been changed over many centuries. For example: *"And you shall call his name Jesus, for he will save his people from their sins" (Matthew 1:21)*. As Yeshua said earlier in the book, "there is no such thing as sin," only "experiencing to learn wisdom." So, why would Yeshua need to save you from sin?

EPILOGUE

Some people have asked me if I wouldn't mind giving a few more details about my life growing up and how I became successful in business, and why did the ascended masters choose me for their messages to be given to those that are willing to listen. Of course, from what I have already written throughout this book about my experiences with Jesus (Yeshua) and the Ascended Masters and with the business world should be enough to allow you to see that it was all about divine guidance and my transitioning into "a sovereign Christ being in my own right." However, I will add just a bit more to what I have already given you by adding this epilogue.

When I was in my early twenties, I did experience the three-dimensional consciousness as far as to whom I believed to be the aspect of Terry, but as soon as the Monks from beyond the physical vail visited me in 1975, that was the beginning of my transitioning to a higher consciousness without me realizing it at the time. Still, during my transition from a three-dimensional consciousness to a fifth-dimensional consciousness and higher, I found myself very mental where everything seemed as if life was perceived as real but, in fact, it was all delusional.

I felt as if I was traveling through some wave-like energy frequency that fostered in something of familiarity to me. It was as if I was causing within myself the ability to distinguish between what was real and what only seemed to be real. Thus, feeling within my heart as if I had the choice to consent to what I was experiencing as being real or to choose to look at it as a distorted state of mind. It was as if my mind was implying that what I was experiencing was a false reality because of it being based on what I believed to be my truths. And, at the same time, it felt that my physical senses were being exposed to an act of trickery on my part because of the belief in two powers.

Therefore, from what I was experiencing, I asked myself, was it false, not real, just an illusion, or was it real? It was as if I had to answer those questions before moving forward with my business, channeling, and with my writings. It was right after my first failure in business and right after praying to God for help when I first realized that something did not feel right to me. And once I allowed myself to let go of what I believed to be God and some Devil after my soul, that is when I felt within me something of familiarity that pushed me over the top when it comes to truth.

My friends, this is how the mind operates, and that is why the Christ within us created this mind. It was to experience life with perception, energy frequency, emotions (false feelings), and how we deal with our choices in order to awaken to a higher part of ourselves that is not the secondary dimensional mental mind or the fourth-dimensional mental mind. Why? Because it does not matter! When looking into the mental part of one's consciousness, no matter what dimension one is at, second, fourth, or higher, it is not about beliefs or thoughts, and that is where many of us have a hard time with our truths and to whom we truly are because we equate consciousness with thoughts and our truths.

Consciousness is beyond time and space, and therefore beyond the mind of thought, beliefs, and fear, since consciousness is what created them in the first place. It is the same when we look at our truths. Why? Because everything linked to our thoughts, beliefs, and fears is all about frequency waves, where we all vibrate at according to those thoughts, beliefs, and fears. For example, suppose you are fixed on a belief (truth) about the education you received in school or what universities imparted to you by your educators as the whole truth and nothing but the truth. In that case, your consciousness frequency drops below the mark of you ever receiving anything to do with your Christ consciousness. It will be the same if you believe that your religion is the pathway to Heaven or that your government is there to guide and protect you.

In other words, if you only see one side of a coin or what you call truth in your eyes as all that is, then you are working from a consciousness frequency that will remove you to any part of your higher consciousness. You see, you are a multidimensional being! Therefore, your consciousness operates on many frequencies at all times, just as radio and TV frequencies, and you do not see those frequencies because you are only tuned into one channel of truth. A truth that was taught to you from birth, leaving out all other channeled frequencies within you. God and the Goddess (your spirit, the "I AM") is within and not outside of you.

Allow me a question: is it your truths that give you real freedom and ascension, or is it your education, emotions, and that of your mind? No to all! Many folks worldwide think about their spiritual path, and yet very few do anything about it. Why? Because very few will allow themselves to move past their already fixed truths to look at the other side of the coin. These people just as soon look at their fellow humans as lost souls because they don't think or believe as they do.

How can you move forward to a fifth-dimensional consciousness and higher, let alone into the fourth dimension where you have the opportunity to choose to either stay in the third dimension of fear or move into the fifth dimension of freedom if you have already made up your mind that your truths are all that there is. Thus, everyone else is wrong! The reason why many of us do not make it to the fourth or fifth dimension and higher is because there are too many distractions that come from our religion, our politics, our education, our family history, and all that the media can pour out to us as their truth.

Many of us work hard to get a bit of information to help us feel secure in what we believe will protect us from getting hurt, losing our money, getting sick, and having plenty of food to eat. And yet, the idea of true freedom escapes our everyday thinking all because of a fear-based consciousness that refuses to look beyond what one is being taught and told without using intuition or common sense. Again, the mask and the virus are a prime example of this!

It is not that the mask itself is going to prevent us from contracting the virus. It is the mask that helps us hide from our true selves because of the fear to move forward in consciousness, which then translates into more illnesses and incarnations. During his time on earth, even Jesus confronted those of leprosy without the fear of contracting it. It saddens Jesus and the ascended masters and myself to see how much the human population, especially those of religious faith and those that feel they are very much in the know, are hypnotized into the belief regarding the understanding of consciousness frequencies.

These people have no idea how "consciousness" plays a part in their evolution to higher frequencies. Thus, who God is and who God isn't then becomes a big question, which is why the book's title is: "You Are Not Who You Believe You Are." Without realizing it, most religious and educational groups commit their energy and consciousness to the dark forces (Devil) without any indication of ever changing their predictable actions in supporting the dark forces that control them.

When we learn to commit to seeing both sides of the coin, that is when we allow ourselves to move forward in consciousness to where we begin to see that over two thousand years ago, the coming of Yeshua Ben Joseph (Jesus) on earth began the New Age movement, as the Christ seed consciousness was planted upon the earth, waiting for its germinating to grab hold now in this lifetime for many. And today, the new age movement has evolved to "New Energy Consciousness," where one has the opportunity to move into the fifth dimension and higher. However, only a few will accept!

Why is that? It is all based on "common sense." We fail to study what is being presented to us as truth from a more intuitive and spiritual way to learn the wisdom behind what is being presented to us as truth. But instead, we work with our minds and our emotions in judging one's perception of facts according to one's training.

In the 1960's it began with channelers like Jane Roberts and others that ultimately raised consciousness to a level where more and more channelers became part of a "New Expanded Consciousness." And today, I am one of those channelers where it has taken me to connect with my "I AM" Christ consciousness and a planet where I have awakened to a consciousness of "I Exist as a Christ and not as a human in need of salvation." Therefore, I am aware of who "I AM" from the Christ level, just as Jesus did when He walked the earth, and not from a mental perception of who Christ is.

This expansion in consciousness goes far beyond a three-dimensional consciousness and that of time, space, and human linear experiences and teachings. It is more than just being birthed, belonging to a church, having an education, having a job, and having a few things in life, and then dying. There is so much more, and it is called ascension, as I call it "freedom," where one's consciousness begins to vibrate at a much higher frequency than a three-dimensional consciousness. Some may call it the fifth-dimensional consciousness and even the Rapture, but in truth, it is just consciousness vibrating at a higher frequency than before.

Envision two standing in a field of a three-dimensional consciousness; one is taken up to the fifth-dimensional consciousness and higher while the other remains in a three-dimensional consciousness, only having to cycle through another twenty-five thousand years of incarnations before the opportunity comes around again. This is the crossroad where some of you are right now, but you fail to wake up from your sleep state due to stubbornness. Therefore, the choice is to be made now and not down the road. And it is all up to you in what you choose!

From living out of a fifth-dimensional consciousness and higher, you are hovering above everything tied to it, which helps you see the happening of things all at once, compared to a three-dimensional consciousness that only sees what is directly in the front of you as truth. Thus, you miss out on many opportunities to help you understand true freedom and how truth, energy, and consciousness expand as you expand.

Everything has opened up to me in this hovering above this very dense three-dimensional consciousness. I can see the dark versus the light and how it is working hard to keep the people and the world in darkness, along with how fear creates the reality we do not want to experience, like the virus for example. It is about being a human versus a divine-human, being young and old, and being in time and out of time, all at the same time.

It is easy for those who choose to stay unawakened and believe that their government, spiritual understanding, health, money, and education will give them the peace and protection they seek, such as a shot protecting them from some virus that does not even exist in the fifth dimension. All of this makes them feel and believe that they are doing something good for society, and yet, all that they are doing is preventing themselves from ascending at least to a fifth-dimensional consciousness.

We are in the age of coming into the realization that we have worked for many lifetimes in bringing in Christ's consciousness and the awareness of knowing the Christ is oneself. I know that only a few will understand this, and for those that don't, it doesn't matter because the few that do will change the outcome of their experiences while they move onto a fifth-dimensional planet and consciousness where peace and fellowship is the norm.

The time of talking about the Rapture has come to an end as of December 21, 2020, and those that are ready to ascend to the fifth-dimensional consciousness and higher will do so through the transitioning of a few years. After that, the split will come to an end, as one will remain behind in a three-dimensional earth while those of ascension will move on to a timeline of at least a fifth-dimensional earth. The only thing left between those that desire to stay with the three-dimensional consciousness of fear and those that are ready to move into this fifth-dimensional frequency is that of allowing them to let go of the old ways God is portrayed, to let go of how we emotionally feel about family members, and to let go of dualness, such as two different forces, that one is either good or bad or that one has to follow group thinking in order to be part of something.

What is really happening right now is that the light is overcoming the dark forces of this earth, and those that refuse to wake up because of their fears will remain in a consciousness of a three-dimensional frequency. We can see it being played out by those that love the dark, such as the mass media, our politicians, our acclaimed celebrities, by those individuals that have the desire to depopulate our planet, and we can see it throughout our religions, our educators, and their followers, as they will not let go of the old teachings.

Our religions have preached to us for centuries about Christ's return, yet they ignore everything tied to the light. For centuries religions of the world have pushed the agenda of the dark forces, and we, the people, believed them and followed them without question. They keep us distracted by selling us on a God that will come and give us salvation if we keep from sinning, not realizing all that they are doing is stealing all that is good from us. Even in their symbols of worship, they call forth the dark forces of evil upon us, and we are too distracted to notice it.

In other words, the disbanding of the dark forces is beginning to move from this planet. And this includes those institutions and individuals who work hard to maintain the dark forces as their energy supply. Therefore, do not be surprised when you see many religious leaders, politicians, educators and their students, governors, mayors, city and county council members, even those in the medical field become exposed to their trickery and all those who work hard to maintain the dark as a way of life for us all.

Because of the planet and some of its people moving into the fifth dimension, they can no longer be part of the earth. Meantime, we will see in many places around the world the dark will try to regroup, but it simply will not work. The example is that of the COVID 19 as being presented to us as something of a consciousness reset. Therefore, it will leave this planet the way it came in, as a lie, because it never existed as proclaimed.

Of course, by the time you have read this book, most of what is being said here about the virus may be starting to let go, or it may be over. However, do not fear, if you happen to be one of those that is still on the fence about what road to travel, then maybe this book will help awaken you from your sleep where you may take the time to do a bit of research into your heart instead of books of a three-dimensional level. Remember, once awakened to the real truth about Christ, God, and the Goddess, all is forgiven!

www.ingramcontent.com/pod-product-compliance
Lightning Source LLC
LaVergne TN
LVHW091545060526
838200LV00036B/705